Open Form
and the Shape of Ideas

Open Form and the Shape of Ideas

Literary Structures
as Representations of Philosophical Concepts
in the Seventeenth and Eighteenth Centuries

Oscar Kenshur

Lewisburg
Bucknell University Press
London and Toronto: Associated University Presses

Associated University Presses
440 Forsgate Drive
Cranbury, NJ 08512

Associated University Presses
25 Sicilian Avenue
London WC1A 2QH, England

Associated University Presses
2133 Royal Windsor Drive
Unit 1
Mississauga, Ontario
Canada L5J 1K5

The paper used in this publication meets the
requirements of the American National Standard for Permanence of Paper
for Printed Library Materials Z39.48-1984.

Library of Congress Cataloging in Publication Data

Kenshur, Oscar, 1942–
  Open form and the shape of ideas.

  Bibliography: p.
  Includes index.
  1. Literature—Philosophy.   2. Literary form.
I. Title.
PN45.K43   1986   809'.93354   84-45458
ISBN 0-8387-5081-8   (alk. paper)

Printed in the United States of America

For my father,
and to the memory of my mother

Contents

Acknowledgments

I am grateful to the following people for reading all or part of the manuscript, in one or more of its versions, and making valuable suggestions: John Hazlett, Raymond Hedin, Donald Marshall, Félix Martínez-Bonati, David Morris, Alan Nagel, and Lee Sterrenburg. Claus Clüver and Josep Sobre graciously helped with the proofreading. Conversations with Deborah Fitzgerald on the role of recognition in concept-formation taught me important things that eventually contributed to my account of visual and quasi-visual representation.

An earlier version of chapter 3 appeared in *Dispositio: Revista Hispánica de Semiótica Literaria* 2 (1977), under the title "Scepticism and the Form of the *Quijote*"; and parts of chapters 1 and 4 appeared in *Papers on Language and Literature* 17 (1981), under the title "Fragments and Order: Two Modern Theories of Discontinuous Form." J. M. Cohen's translations from the *Quijote* are reprinted here with the permission of Penguin Books.

Open Form
and the Shape of Ideas

1

The Nature and Interpretation of Open Forms

"If there's no meaning in it," said the King, "that saves a world
of trouble, you know, as we needn't try to find any."
—Lewis Carroll, *Alice in Wonderland*

Preliminary

The primary task of this study is to examine some of the ways in
which discontinuous literary forms of the seventeenth and eighteenth centuries serve as representations of philosophical ideas.
Although there have previously been piecemeal efforts in this direction, most scholars, and particularly those concerned with
modern literature, apparently continue to adhere to the belief that
discontinuous literary works—works whose gaps, whether logical,
narrative, grammatical, or typographical, prevent the separate
parts from combining into unified wholes—constitute a distinctly
modern phenomenon that somehow reflects modern views about
the world. The persistence of this belief seems attributable, at least
in part, to the fact that accounts of the phenomenon tend to
characterize it in terms—such as fragmentation and ambiguity—
that are associated with modern literature and thought. The concepts of ambiguity and fragmentation, however, are invoked more
often than they are analyzed, and although their invocation is tied
to assumptions about the interpretation or interpretability of literary texts, these assumptions also tend to go unacknowledged and
unexamined. Thus the claim that one is dealing with a specifically
modern phenomenon is not simply an historical claim, but is also,
at least implicitly, a theoretical one; and any attempt to evaluate the
claim must therefore proceed along both historical and theoretical
lines. Accordingly, although this study of discontinuous forms is
intended to be a contribution to the literary and intellectual history

of the seventeenth and eighteenth centuries, it cannot identify and situate the historical phenomenon under consideration without also engaging the theory of discontinuous form. Toward this end, it will be convenient to use as a point of departure two prominent and contrasting accounts of modern discontinuous forms, those of Umberto Eco and Joseph Frank. Our concern will be less with the actual historical phenomena that these writers are attempting to describe than with the theoretical implications of their descriptions.

Open Work and Spatial Form

Eco's conception of the *opera aperta*[1] is that of a distinctly modern phenomenon, a class of avant-garde discontinuous works marked by (1) a fragmentary form that serves as an "epistemological metaphor," reflecting the way in which contemporary culture views reality; and (2) an ambiguous relationship between its fragmentary parts. The ambiguity of an open work, according to Eco, is indicated by the special role of the interpreter, the special degree to which she or he is presented with the task of completing the artist's work. Eco grants that all art is in a sense open, since all art is interpreted by its consumer. But he nonetheless sees a difference between works that are formally closed and those that formally require the interpreter to close them.[2] An open work not only demands more of its consumers, but it demands it perpetually. The consumer's task is not merely to choose a meaning from among a limited number of alternatives, nor to assimilate such alternatives, reconciling them with one another. The open work is seen as "a continuous potentiality of 'openness,' in other words, an indefinite reserve of meanings."[3]

The reason that the open work can be recognized as an inexhaustible store of possible interpretations lies, it seems, in its form. In verbal ambiguities of the sort that William Empson describes in his celebrated study,[4] possible meanings are apparently recognized one after another. One may not be certain, at any given moment, that all possible meanings have been discovered, but neither, presumably, can one be certain that there are further possible meanings left to be discovered. Ambiguity is discovered only as each alternative meaning is recognized. The number of apparent meanings is limited, and the reader mentally orders them, perhaps on the basis of their relative plausibility or their mutual compatibility.

This applies to ambiguity arising from discontinuity as well as to other sorts:

> two statements are made as if they were connected, and the reader is forced to consider their relations for himself. The reason why these facts should have been selected for a poem is left for him to invent; he will invent a variety of reasons and order them in his own mind.[5]

Eco's open work, on the other hand, has a form that in itself seems to proclaim its inexhaustible supply of meanings. The form of the work itself seems to exclude univocality and to proclaim itself as a "champ de possibilités."[6] The form is a discontinuous one, and the reason one recognizes it as a field of possibilities is apparently that its discontinuity leaves the arrangement of the elements more or less up to the interpreter. One of Eco's paradigms is Stockhausen's *Klavierstück XI*, which requires the musician to "choose among . . . [note] groupings, first for the one to start the piece and, next, for the successive units in the order in which he elects to weld them together." Eco continues his description thus:

> In this type of performance, the instrumentalist's freedom is a function of the "combinative" structure of the piece, which allows him to "mount" the sequence of musical units in the order he chooses.[7]

This interpretability, founded on a discontinuous form, is what Eco seems to mean by "ambiguity."

The source of ambiguity in Eco's open work thus lies in the fact that the relationship between a series of discrete elements that constitute a given work is indeterminate and that it is consequently left to the interpreter to determine the web of relationships. Since the possible combinations may be virtually infinite, and the reader has no clue as to how the elements ought to be arranged, he is left with a number of possible interpretations, none of which can be validated.

The first thing to be noted about the ambiguity of the open work is that while it characterizes the relationship between the parts, it does not apply to the signification of the whole. We have already noted that the open work functions to represent epistemological attitudes. Artistic form in general, Eco observes, may serve as an epistemological metaphor:

> In every century the way that artistic forms are structured reflects the way in which science or contemporary culture views reality.[8]

Modern discontinuous forms, for example, may reflect such scientific principles as those of indeterminacy and complementarity. For open works of art, as for models that contradict one another while serving a heuristic function: "an incomplete knowledge of the system is in fact an essential feature in its formulation."[9] Thus the incompleteness, or lack of closure, in a work of art can be an essential feature, reflecting the incompleteness of our knowledge and even the necessity of such incompleteness. In one of the more interesting formulations of its mode of representation, the open work becomes something like a Kantian transcendental schema:

> Tout cela éclaire la fonction d'un art nouveau comme métaphore épistémologique. La discontinuité des phénomèmes remet en question la possibilité d'une image unifiée et définitive de l'univers; l'art nous propose un moyen de nous représenter ce même monde, le monde où nous vivons, et, ce faisant, de l'accepter, de l'intégrer à notre sensibilité. L'oeuvre "ouverte" entend en pleine lucidité donner une image de la discontinuité: elle ne la raconte pas, elle *est* cette discontinuité. Elle se pose en *médiatrice*, entre les catégories de la science et la matière vivante de notre sensibilité; c'est comme une sorte de schéma transcendental qui nous permet de saisir de nouveaux aspects du monde.[10]

> All this throws light on the function of open art as an epistemological metaphor. The discontinuity of phenomena puts into question the possibility of a unified and definitive picture of the universe; such art offers us a mode of representing to ourselves the actual world in which we live, and thereby of coming to terms with it, of integrating it into our own consciousness. The "open" work conscientiously undertakes to provide an image of discontinuity: it does not tell us about this discontinuity; it *is* this discontinuity. It takes on the role of a mediator between the categories of science and the living stuff of our consciousness; it is like a sort of transcendental schema that allows us to grasp new aspects of the world.

Now, whichever formulation we employ in describing the relationship between the open work and external reality, or our modes of apprehending external reality, it seems clear that for Eco this relationship is not ambiguous. That is, the fact that the discontinuous form of the open work signifies something about our cognition of the world is not merely one of a number of possible interpretations of this discontinuous form, but is apparently the single correct interpretation of it. In short, while the relationship between the elements of the open work is ambiguous, this ambiguity is itself significant, and univocally so.

Although this formulation of Eco's view sounds paradoxical, it is possible to suppose that Eco would not find the paradox disquieting or damaging to his position. Why, he might ask, should it not be perfectly possible for a whole that is characterized by an ambiguous relationship between its parts to have, *qua* indeterminate whole, a univocal signification? It is this rhetorical question that now needs to be answered.

The most convenient way for us to determine whether Eco's conception of the open work's paradoxical mode of signification is in fact a coherent one is by means of a consideration of what is required in order for the reader to be able to recognize the univocal signification of the entire text. What allows the reader to determine that the open work signifies something about our inability to achieve a fixed and objective knowledge of external reality? The immediate precondition for this act of interpretation is clearly the recognition that the text is so structured as to imitate or enact or otherwise indicate the epistemological barriers that stand between us and objective knowledge. To interpret in this way, the reader must be able to recognize that the open structure is an intrinsic feature of the work. If the reader finds himself presented with a number of discontinuous elements whose interrelationships need to be established, and if, in search of the correct configuration, he persists in trying one possibility after another, then he will presumably remain in error about the nature of the text. He will fail to recognize that there is no single set of relationships that is correct or adequate. For if a demonstrably adequate set of relationships could be found and imposed on the disparate elements, then the text would have proved to be a mere puzzle whose amenability to solution had deprived it of the radical epistemological signification that, according to Eco, characterizes the open work. It would not in fact be an open work, according to Eco's definition.

It will be seen then that in order for the reader to be able to interpret the open structure, to discover its meaning *qua* open structure, it will be necessary not merely that he fail to find an adequate set of relationships, but that he recognize that it is fruitless to search for such relationships. He must, in short, expect neither that the text will provide a key to the relationship between its elements nor that he will be able to supplement the text by providing the key himself.

Now, if we do not expect an explanation, then we are not troubled by its absence, and if a text does not provide fewer explanations than we expect of it, it is not ambiguous. The conditions for ambiguity are in fact frustrated expectations, and a text's failure to connect its elements to one another is ambiguous only when such a connection is expected. To substantiate this claim—in case it requires substantiation—we need only consider the case of ambiguity at the level of the sentence. At first glance, the sentence seems to provide a paradigm to support Eco's claim that a discontinuous form is ambiguous. For if a sentence is discontinuous, if, that is, it has syntactic gaps that obscure the relationship between its elements, then it will indeed be ambiguous. But in order for such ambiguity to occur, we first need to recognize the group of words as a sentence. For if we see a group of words as something other than a sentence, for example, as a list, then the lack of complete sentential syntax will not strike us as ambiguous. In other words, if we do not see a group of words as a sentence we shall not expect the syntactic relations that obtain in a sentence, and their absence, consequently, will not result in ambiguity. By the same token, since a correct interpretation of the significance of Eco's open structure requires that there be no expectations with regard to the relationship between the parts, once we recognize an open work to be an open work, the relationship between its parts necessarily becomes unambiguous.[11]

The notion of ambiguity that I have been ascribing to Eco is essentially one in which the relationship between the parts is "underdetermined," in which, that is, the context fails to authorize any of the possible relationships between the parts. It might be objected, however, that this ascription is unfair, and that Eco, in fact, sees the ambiguity of the open work as overdetermined, an ambiguity, that is, in which the relationships between the parts is determinate, but in which more than one combination is authorized. And indeed Eco sometimes characterizes the open work as "plurivoque," suggesting that it sustains more than one meaning simultaneously. To grant this, however, is not to grant that Eco is really positing the ambiguity of overdetermination, or even that such a position could save his account. For although Eco states that the open work is "plurivoque," he does not actually describe its mode of signification in terms of multiple meanings simultaneously sustained. Rather, he talks of "champs de possibilité" and "la liberté de l'interprète." And indeed, if we try to understand the open work in terms of the authorization of multiple combinations, the weight of Eco's own pronouncements would require that we see this overdetermination as one in which *all* possible combinations of the elements are equally authorized, insofar as none may be deemed incorrect. But such an "overdetermined" mode of signification would, in an important sense, be identical to that found in the ambiguity of underdetermination. The notion that more than one reading is positively authorized would seem to depend on the presence of other readings that are not authorized, that are incorrect. But when *all* possible readings are equally authorized, then the distinction between the presence of multiple authorization and the absence of any authorization collapses: the overdetermined becomes indistinguishable from the underdetermined. Thus the problem of reconciling the structural significance of the open work with its supposed structural ambiguity is not resolved by the invocation of any second sort of ambiguity.[12]

I have been at pains to point out the error in Eco's account not because I think that he is describing something that cannot exist, but because I think that he is simply misdescribing something that does exist, namely, the open form that is the subject of the present study. And my analysis of that error has been adding, albeit in a negative way, to a correct description of the actual phenomenon. For the open form's lack of ambiguity indicates, in fact, one of its fundamental characteristics. It is worth making this more explicit, even at the risk of repeating myself. I have said that the significance of the open work can be recognized only when we recognize that the relationship between its discontinuous parts is not syntactic. This precludes the possibility of overdetermined ambiguity as well as the underdetermined sort. The syntax of a macrostructure, like that of a sentence, positively establishes the relationship between the elements, and hence the meaning. In underdetermined ambiguity, more than one relationship seems possible, but none is authorized. There is a failure to establish positively the relationship between the elements. In overdetermined ambiguity, more than one combination is positively established. But the open work achieves its signification precisely by a sort of "negative grammar," a clear refusal to establish *any* syntactic relationship between the discontinuous elements. It is only when we recognize that this negative grammar is in operation that the discontinuous parts are able, in Eco's terms, "donner une image de la discontinuité." The open work, that is, calls attention to the fact that what is operative is not a linguistic or quasi-linguistic linking of verbal elements, and hence a conceptual linking of their referents, but a sort of quasi-visual representation by the discontinuous structure itself. We are not puzzled as to how to put together fragments of meaning if we recognize that the text's meaning is to be a picture of fragments.

I have said that Eco's open work has a mode of signification that involves a quasi-visual representation on the part of the overall discontinuous structure, and that in order for this signification to occur, the structural configuration must be unambiguously recognizable as such. (Later in this chapter, I will be more precise about what I mean by saying that the open work serves as a "quasi-visual" representation. Meanwhile, I trust that, even without such elucidation, my usage is intelligible.) But if my critique of Eco's analysis moves us in the direction of a correct definition of the phenomenon with which the present study is concerned, it by no means provides us with an adequate understanding of this phenomenon. If an open work demands that we not attempt to unify its discontinuous parts, but that we look at the assemblage of parts as a sort of visual configuration, then how do we recognize that this demand is being made of us? How do we know, that is, that we are not supposed to try to put the parts back together? How, in short, do we know that we are reading an open work?

What I have already said about ambiguity implies a possible answer to this question. I have noted that while a lack of clarity in the syntactic relationships between the elements of a sentence rendered that sentence ambiguous, our recognition of the same group of words as a list rather than a sentence might remove all ambiguity. By the same token, if we recognize a text as a Greek tragedy, then we expect certain kinds of relationships, namely, causal relationships between a series of described events, and gaps in this causal chain would cause ambiguity. However, if we do not take a given text to be a Greek tragedy, then the absence of a chain of causal explanations might not strike us as ambiguous. These examples are typical. All our expectations regarding the types of relationships that will be drawn between the elements of a text are in fact determined by the type of text that we take it to be. This applies to all texts or utterances, not merely those belonging to conventional literary types. Thus a sentence, like a tragedy, can represent a type. In spite of the wide range of types into which utterances may be classed, it will be convenient, following E. D. Hirsch, to replace the term *type* with the term *genre*.[13]

Since we conventionally tend to look first for the referential dimension in verbal discourse, we do not, according to this analysis, think to notice the representational aspect of the form until we determine that the relationship between the parts of the discourse does not follow the normal referential pattern for a given genre, until, that is, our generic expectations have been violated. Open works, then, would establish their status as open works by distinguishing themselves from closed literary (or philosophical) genres, and thus by replacing one set of generic expectations with another. Insofar as a text proclaims its status as an open work by distinguishing itself from a closed genre, it represents a sort of *countergenre;*[14] and it may well be the case that a recognition of this countergeneric status is a precondition for recognizing an open work.

But this generic or countergeneric account of how we recognize open works, however attractive it may be, is unfortunately inadequate. For the fact that a discontinuous work serves as a countergenre is not sufficient to assure that the reader will, or ought to, see the discontinuous structural configuration as representational. Indeed, one of the most influential accounts of modern discontinuous forms, that of Joseph Frank, begins, in effect, with a recognition of their countergeneric status, but then, instead of urging us to look at the discontinuous configuration as a representation, offers a prescription for reassembling the discontinuous parts. Frank's way of looking at discontinuous works is in fact so strikingly different from Eco's that a comparison between the two theories will be instructive.

Just as fragments are a precondition for the *opera aperta*'s role as a metaphor for modern philosophical outlooks, fragments are also a precondition for the emergence of Frank's "spatial form."[15] According to Frank, when the continuity that characterizes conventional literary discourse is broken up, or fragmented, then we are no longer able to apprehend a work as a continuous temporal sequence. But whereas Eco's open works point to the arbitrariness of all attempted reconstructions of the fragments, and hence to the function of the collection of fragments as an epistemological metaphor, Frank's fragments, after "frustrating the reader's normal expectations of a sequence, [force] him to perceive the elements . . . as juxtaposed in space rather than as unrolling in time."[16] And what the reader perceives is not a series of fragments, but an organization that transcends them. After recognizing that, in terms of the temporal order in which the text is presented to us, it is fragmented, we, as it were, spread the fragments out before us all at once, and put them together in a new order. Or, as Frank puts it, with specific reference to Joyce, "These references [the disconnected references to Dublin life presented in *Ulysses*] must be connected by the reader and viewed as a whole before the book fits together in any meaningful pattern."[17] This procedure of organizing the fragments independently of the temporal order in which they were given is what Frank is talking about when he claims that for readers of "spatial" works, "temporal" apprehension is replaced by "spatial" apprehension.

Frank's notion of spatial form has often been called formalistic, and, indeed, there is considerable justification for the use of the term. When disconnected from one another, the parts of a spatial work, the fragments, do not refer directly to external reality, but rather to one another:

> Instead of the instinctive and immediate reference of words and word-groups to the objects or events they symbolize and the construction of meaning from the sequence of these references, modern poetry asks its readers to suspend the process of individual reference temporarily until the entire pattern of internal references can be apprehended as a unity.[18]

In this sense spatial works are "reflexive" rather than "referential," and the pattern that emerges when we recombine the various pieces recalls the aesthetic patterns that we associate with formalism. Frank does not in fact claim that the unified pattern that results from the reconstruction of the fragmentary parts into a new whole precludes any referentiality of the whole to an external state of affairs. Indeed, "to suspend the process of individual reference temporarily" does not necessitate our suspending it ultimately. Frank tells us that in *Ulysses,* for example, the putting together of the fragments ultimately yields a "picture of Dublin seen as a whole."[19] There thus seems to be a referential dimension to spatiality, or at least the possibility of one.

But what is crucial is clearly not the fact of referentiality, but the mode of referentiality. For spatial form, with its suspension of referentiality until the whole is assembled and apprehended in a moment of time, is likened by Frank to the abstract forms of modern art, and both are seen as attempts to overcome the insecurity and instability of modern life by achieving the timeless state of myth.[20] What matters then is not the accurate representation of reality but the transcendence of reality by means of artistic form. As Frank says of Djuna Barnes's *Nightwood*, "We are asked only to accept the work of art as an autonomous structure . . . and the question of the relation of this vision to an extra-artistic 'objective' world has ceased to have any fundamental importance."[21]

The difference between Eco's *opera aperta* then, when it is freed from the claim that it is ambiguous, and Frank's notion of spatial

form, seems to resolve itself into a version of the traditional opposition between art as a representation of reality and art as an escape
from or an improvement upon reality. The form of an open work is
properly seen by its reader as consisting of disconnected and un-
connectable fragments that represent reality as it is interpreted by
modern science and epistemology. A spatial work, on the other
hand, is properly seen as a timeless formal structure that transcends the imperfections of reality.[22] But underlying this difference
is a similarity to which I have already adverted: both open works
and spatial forms manifest a prima facie disorder that initially frus-
trates the reader's conventional expectations; both, that is to say,
have a countergeneric relationship to traditional closed forms. This
being the case, the recognition of the countergeneric relationship
cannot, in itself, tell us whether a given discontinuous work is an
open work or a spatial form.

Now, it might be supposed that once the countergeneric status
of a given discontinuous form has been recognized, one could
ascertain whether it is an open work or a spatial form—assuming
that those are the only possibilities—simply by looking to see
whether it has the attributes of one sort of text or the other. But in
fact, although I have no inclination to dispute Eco's claim that
there is a class of open works, or Frank's claim that there are spatial
forms, I am obliged to note that, in principle, *any* discontinuous
work could be read either as an open work or as a spatial form. For
both approaches depend upon the recognition of resemblances,
and resemblances can always be found.

That the open work's role as an epistemological metaphor depends upon resemblances is acknowledged by Eco fairly explicitly,
particularly in the French version (*L'Oeuvre ouverte*, p. 28):

> la manière dont se structurent les diverses formes d'art révèle—*au sens
> large, par similitude, métaphore, résolution du concept en figure*—la
> manière dont la science ou, en tout cas, la culture contemporaine
> voient la réalité.[23] (Italics mine)

> The way that the various artistic forms are structured reveals—*in the
> broadest sense, by simile, by metaphor, by the figural rendering of con-
> cepts*—the way in which science or, in any event, contemporary cul-
> ture, views reality.

But it is not so much the specific formulations as the entire tenor
and logic of Eco's account—which, I trust, has been reflected in
my brief summary—that leads us to the conclusion that the opera-

tion by which a discontinuous form uses "une image de la discontinuité" to signify the ideas of modern physics and epistemology involves a resemblance between the form and the ideas.

In the case of Frank, the role of resemblances is less explicit, but equally inescapable. Here, however, the resemblances are not between the structural configuration and something external to it, but are to be found among the discontinuous parts themselves, or more precisely, aspects of those parts. For in the absence of the sequential continuity that Frank associates with traditional literature, the spatialization, the reunification, of the fragmented parts must, as far as I can tell, depend on resemblances between them.

The fact that there are always resemblances to be found between any two things, or among any group of things, has become a commonplace of contemporary discussions of representation,[24] and has often been adduced to support the claim that representation, at the very least, cannot be accounted for strictly by appeal to a resemblance between the representation and its object. Nor need we appeal to any particular theory of representation in order to be able to point out that our capacity to find a resemblance between a discontinuous literary structure and an idea is by no means sufficient warrant for claiming that the structure *represents* that idea or set of ideas, or that it represents anything at all. Therefore the ability to find such a resemblance does not allow us to ascertain that we are dealing with an open work.

The same ease with which we can find resemblances between the structural configuration of a discontinuous work and something external to it also obtains in the search for resemblances between the parts of such a work. Indeed, since those who purport to find unity in apparently disunified works rarely specify, except in an ad hoc fashion, what sorts of resemblances constitute unity, their attempts to find unifying resemblances can scarcely fail.[25] In short, since resemblances among parts can always be found, it is always possible to claim that any assemblage is "unified."[26]

Since one can always find resemblances among discontinuous parts, and since one can always find a resemblance between a configuration of discontinuous parts and something else (such as an epistemological theory arising from quantum physics) one can, as I have said, read any discontinuous text either as a spatial form or as an open work. How, then, to reformulate the crucial question that I posed above, can we determine, when confronted with a discontinuous work, that it is appropriate not to undertake to find unifying resemblances, but to do what we shall be doing in the next several chapters, namely, looking at the overall discontinuous configuration as an image of ideas?

The question then is not, "Which resemblance can we find?" but rather "Which resemblances are we supposed to find?" And the answer will have to involve at least one element beyond the resemblance, namely, the context or contexts that control or confirm our recognition of resemblances.

Visual Representation and the Interpretation of Open Forms

A paradigmatic example of the role of contexts in the interpretation of resemblances is to be found in Bacon's *Novum Organum*. The work will be discussed at length in chapter 2, but it will be useful briefly to refer ahead to an aspect of that discussion.

The *Novum Organum* is an aphoristic work that proposes an inductive method that Bacon claims will allow us to move from the disparate facts of experience to a comprehensive knowledge of the natural world. In the eighty-sixth aphorism of Book I of the *Novum Organum*, Bacon contrasts the aphoristic form with forms that set science

> forth with such ambition and parade, and bring them into the view of the world so fashioned and masked as if they were complete in all parts and finished.

Such forms, unlike aphoristic ones consisting of "short and scattered sentences not linked together by an artificial method," retard the pursuit of learning because they give the impression that knowledge is complete:

> it is nothing strange if men do not seek to advance in things delivered to them as long since perfect and complete.[27]

My preliminary interpretation of the form of the *Novum Organum*, accordingly, will see it as a representation of the fragmentary state of scientific knowledge, or what Bacon elsewhere referred to as "knowledge broken."[28] Such an interpretation will probably strike the reader as no more ingenious than, say, an interpretation of Rembrandt's *Aristotle Contemplating the Bust of Homer* that sees the painting as a representation of Aristotle contemplating the bust of Homer. It is this exegetical straightforwardness that gives the *Novum Organum* its paradigmatic character. But in order for the interpretation of the work to be able to serve as a paradigm for the interpretations of other works, we need to be able to specify those characteristics which seem to make the work particularly interpretable and which render our interpretation plausible.

In the light of what I have said thus far, one might suppose that the interpretability of the work depends upon Bacon's pronouncements about the representational function of the aphoristic form. But it is possible to interpret Bacon's own pronouncements as describing the interpretive situation without being essential to it. Thus the pronouncements would suggest analyses that, paradoxically, render the pronouncements themselves superfluous.

On the one hand Bacon may be seen to be suggesting that the aphoristic form is inherently fragmentary, and that its capacity to represent fragments is therefore intrinsic: it represents fragments because it is itself fragmentary. If this were true, then there would be no need of Bacon's own pronouncements to serve a contextual function. But aphorisms, like other discontinuous forms, are not *ipso facto* fragments. To see the parts of a discontinuous work as fragments is to see them in terms of the dichotomy of parts versus wholes, where the lack of connection is tantamount to fragmentation. But as we shall see, there are other possible frameworks, such as the dichotomy of chaos versus order, in which chaos is marked by undifferentiated unity, and order consists of discrete parts (see chapter 4 below); or the dichotomy of realism versus nominalism, in which a world made up of classes whose members share essences is contrasted with a world of ontological individuation (see chapters 2 and 5 below). The claim that discontinuous forms are intrinsically fragmentary and that they naturally represent fragmentary things is, in fact, an extreme version of the erroneous claim that the resemblance that one happens to notice is necessarily operative. For in this case the resemblance that one notices is not even recognized to be a mere resemblance; resemblance is confused with identity, metaphor with reality. (That this confusion is easy to fall into is evidenced by the fact that it is the point of agreement between such otherwise disparate theorists as Frank and Eco.)

Moreover, even if a discontinuous form *were* inherently fragmentary, that would still not imply that it naturally represented fragmentary things. To be a member of a given class of things is not necessarily to be a representation of other members of that class. A chair is not normally a representation of other chairs, and a painting of a chair, while a representation of chairs, is not a representation of other paintings. (This disjunction between what something exemplifies and what it represents has already been encountered in Frank's notion of spatial form. For although he assumes—too hastily, as it turns out—that spatial forms are inherently fragmentary, Frank, unlike Eco, does not see this as implying that the forms have representational functions.)

The second alternative account that one could elicit from Bacon's pronouncements would not center on any allegedly intrinsic fragmentariness of aphorisms, but on their conventional significance. Ernst Gombrich has provided substantial empirical evidence to demonstrate that, in the visual arts, we often determine what is being represented insofar as we recognize a given work as belonging to a traditional mode of representation.[29] Thus we recognize that a picture represents a tree because we recognize the picture as adhering to a traditional mode of representing trees. Similarly, it could be argued that when Bacon claims that aphorisms represent knowledge broken, he is appealing, not to an intrinsic resemblance between aphorisms and fragmentary knowledge, but to a generic convention according to which aphorisms represent epistemological fragmentation. And such a convention might seem to provide us with a determining context that would allow us to ascertain which resemblance is operative. Indeed, it might even be argued that the concept of a representational convention might allow us to do without the resemblance between the representation and its object. For if the members of a given representational tradition have a certain representational significance, and one can recognize that a given work belongs to that tradition, then it might seem that such recognition would be sufficient to establish the representational significance of the work.

In response to such a suggestion, it needs to be noted that we recognize that an individual discontinuous work belongs to a given genre by recognizing the resemblance between the work and other works making up the same genre. Since the recognition of a genre depends on the recognition of resemblances, it would seem to be subject to the same difficulties that we have found in the case of the interpretation of representations. That is, in principle, more than one resemblance, and hence more than one genre, may be found, and we need a further context to allow us to determine which resemblance is operative. And if the number of literary genres is sufficiently small to render confusion unlikely, our discussion of Eco and Frank has demonstrated that, with respect to discontinuous forms, two divergent possibilities are sufficient to cause difficulties. For if the generic markings of the open form and the spatial form are the same, then the appeal to generic conventions is not going to be adequate to allow us to determine that a given discontinuous text is an open work, let alone that it represents this or that. In short, however useful the concept of representational conventions may be, it cannot be sufficient to allow us to recognize and interpret open forms.

Having set aside these alternatives, we are in a position to see what is paradigmatic about Bacon's text. Once we recognize that Bacon's pronouncements do not point to any immediately identifiable feature of aphorisms by virtue of which they naturally or conventionally represent fragmentary knowledge, we are left with the possibility that the representational meaning of the form depends on the pronouncements themselves. But this is not to say that the form can represent anything that Bacon says it represents. On the contrary, the actual situation is analogous to that in the visual arts. But before we can see how this is the case, it will be useful to add a bit more precision to my earlier claim that the open form is a quasi-visual configuration.

Although an aphoristic work in which the individual aphorisms are set off from one another by means of typographical spaces, or a poem that is set in such a way as to give it the shape of an altar or of a diamond adds a visual component to its form, literary form is, for the most part, something that we establish not by looking at a literary work, but by reading it. Thus, although the discontinuity of an open work may be established partly by its physical presentation or format, most of the formal elements that yield discontinuity are not things that we literally see. An open novel, for example, need not look different from any other novel, but will contain a discontinuity that is established by digressions, or episodic fragmentation of the narrative, or the absence of causal explanations, or the disjointing of chronology, or any one of a number of other possible features that will be functions not only of the way that fictional events are described and related to one another, but even of the nature of those fictional events themselves. Insofar as the discontinuity of a work is a function of the lack of an explanation for the occurrence of an event, or the lack of motivation for an action, or a temporal gap between actions, literary form is not only something that we do not see, but it is a function of "content." But this no more precludes resemblance than does the situation in which the thing being represented is itself not visual.

The aphoristic form, for example, may be seen to resemble a state of knowledge in which there are isolated facts and observations but no comprehensive explanations to tie them together; yet neither pole of the resemblance is something visible. In the case of the *Novum Organum*, there are, to be sure, typographical gaps between the aphorisms, but these visual spaces are not essential to the resemblance. The aphorisms could be presented as consecutive paragraphs without any visual breaks between them and the disconnectedness could be established by lack of logical or grammatical connectives between the paragraphs. The fragmented knowledge that the aphoristic form resembles, in any case, is not something visual. Nonetheless the resemblance is real. The state of knowledge that Bacon describes is like the aphoristic form insofar as both consist of a field of isolated entities that are understood to be disconnected from one another. Now, it is possible that our recognition of the resemblance between the two things is facilitated by the fact that both can be visualized in similar or even identical ways. Thus the resemblance could be mediated by a single picture that resembles both poles—disconnected knowledge and aphoristic form. Indeed, the language with which we describe the two resembling things tends to be the same because the metaphoricity of language implicitly results in comparing even the most abstract things to some concrete exemplar. Thus the aphorisitic form and early seventeenth-century scientific knowledge may both be termed "fragmentary" insofar as both may be seen to resemble, say, the scattered shards of a broken pot. For my purposes, however, it is not necessary to delineate the mechanisms of resemblance, or to fix the role of the visual in the resemblance of abstract things to some concrete exemplar. Thus the aphoristic form and knowledge through the mediation of a *tertium quid,* a visible or concrete thing, or through direct comparison on the conceptual level, the role of the resemblance in our interpretation of literary open form is unaffected. And I submit that whether implicitly visual or purely conceptual, the resemblance between a given open form and something else is quasi-visual to the extent that it has the same role in our determination of what is being represented as the resemblance between a strictly visual configuration on a canvas and, say, Henry VIII. For in both cases any resemblance between the configuration and something else is not adequate to establish the representational significance, and in both cases the determining contexts are the ones that we take to be informed by the artist's intentions.

The interpretive situation in the visual arts has recently been aptly described by Richard Wollheim:

> What is unique to the seeing appropriate to representations is this: that a standard of correctness applies to it and this standard derives from the intention of the maker of the representation, or the "artist," as he is usually called. . . . Naturally the standard of correctness cannot require that someone should see a particular representation in a particular way if even a fully informed and competent spectator could not see it in that way. What the standard does is to select the correct perception of a representation out of possible perceptions of it, where possible perceptions are those open to spectators in possession of all the relevant skills and beliefs. If, through the incompetence, ignorance, or bad luck of the artist, the possible perceptions of a given representation do not include one that matches the artist's intention, there is, for that representation, no correct perception—and consequently . . . nothing or no one represented.[30]

By way of showing how these standards operate in practice, and to aid us in seeing just how the recognition of representations in the visual arts relates to the recognition and interpretation of open forms, it will be useful to consider Wollheim's own examples:

> In a certain sixteenth-century engraving, ascribed to a follower of Marcantonio, some art-historians have seen a dog curled up asleep at the feet of a female saint. Closer attention to the subject, and to the print itself, will show the spectator that the animal is a lamb. In Holbein's famous portrait in three-quarters view (coll. Thyssen) I normally see Henry VIII. However, I may have been going to too many old movies recently, and I look at the portrait and, instead of seeing Henry VIII, I now find myself seeing Charles Laughton. In each of these two cases there is a standard that says that one of the perceptions is correct and the other incorrect, this standard goes back to the intentions of the unknown engraver or of Holbein, and, in so far as I set myself to look at the representation as a representation, I must try to get my perception to conform to this standard. However, if the unknown engraver had shown himself unable to draw a lamb, and so no lamb could be made out in the print, or if Holbein had failed to portray Henry VIII . . . and, accordingly, Henry VIII was not visible in the painting, then the standard would not require me to see in one case a lamb, in the other case Henry VIII, nor would there be a correct perception of either work.[31]

Now, in claiming that Wollheim's description of the interpretation of visual representations applies to the interpretation of liter-

ary open forms, I come close to the brink of a philosophical prec-
ipice. If there is a "standard of correctness" that is tied to the
maker's intentions, does that mean that representational meanings
are real entities that are called into being by the maker's will, and
that correctness is a matter of correspondence between our interpretations and those entities?[32] Such a question summons up a host
of issues in the theory of meaning and the philosophy of mind, as
well as more general issues of metaphysics and epistemology—
issues that cannot be dealt with here. But I think that the applicability of Wollheim's remarks can be established without our having
to plunge into these treacherous philosophical waters.

Wollheim's description of the interpretation of visual representations, I submit, implicitly rests on the distinction that we make, in
ordinary language, between fortuitous resemblances and representations. If I notice a resemblance between a cloud and, say, a
camel, and remark to an acquaintance,

Do you see that cloud that's almost in shape like a camel?

the acquaintance might recognize the resemblance, but would not
decide that the cloud was a *representation* of a camel. For we do
not consider something to be a representation unless someone has
made it. This is a cultural fact, independent of the question of what
sort of ontological commitment might or might not be entailed by
this fact. Now, it is important to recognize that this concept of
representation, as it is enshrined in our language, includes in it a
certain principle of interpretation. For it is possible that even a
made object may be seen to resemble something else, without our
considering it to be a representation. For example, we may look at
the handlebars of a bicycle and recognize both that they are made
and that they may be seen to resemble a bull's horns; but we will
nonetheless not normally consider the handlebars a representation
of a bull's horns. For in this case, as in the case of the cloud, we
consider the resemblance to be merely fortuitous; and a made
object that bears a fortuitous resemblance to something is in itself
no more a representation than is a natural object that bears a fortuitous resemblance to something. To consider something a representation, we require not merely that the object be made, but that
the *resemblance be made,* that is, that the object be made *qua*
resemblance.[33] And, of course, another way of saying this is that in
order for something to be a representation, the resemblance must
be intended.

Thus the concept of visual representation includes the concept of artistic intention, and although the cultural situation in which we are presented with representations in frames, on museum walls, on pedestals, and so on, tends to separate phenomenologically the recognition of an object's status as a representation from the interpretation of its representational significance, they are not separate procedures in principle. Indeed, if we were called upon to do without such "prepackaging," our recognition that an object is a representation would necessarily be simultaneous with our recognition that it was a "made resemblance" of this or that. Thus our recognition that something is a representation would be simultaneous with our interpretation of it.

It is in this sense that Wollheim's account of the interpretive situation is simply an explication of our concept of representation. To require a match between a possible perception (or what I have been calling a "possible resemblance") and the maker's intention is not simply to recommend an interpretive procedure; it is to remind us of what is needed in order to have a representation in the first place. If we keep in mind that a representation is a made resemblance, then it will be easy to gauge the role of contexts in our interpretive procedure. Contextual evidence is relevant to the extent that it allows us to conclude that a given object is or is not a made resemblance. Thus Bacon's remarks about the representational significance of the aphoristic form constitute relevant evidence with respect to the representational significance of the *Novum Organum* because Bacon is the author of the work and because the form of the work is adequate to the representational function that he ascribes to it—that is, because the form indeed includes among its possible resemblances one that is adequate to the maker's intentions. In the case of an open form, as in the case of a painting of Henry VIII, the form must resemble the intended object to the extent that we can see (or conceive) it as an image (or formal analogue) of that object. If Bacon had declared that the form of the *Novum Organum* represented epistemological fragmentation, but we could perceive no resemblance between the form of the work and the fragmentary state of scientific knowledge, then, to paraphrase Wollheim, the possible perceptions of the form could not include one that matches the artist's intention, and there would be nothing represented.

Of course the possibility that nothing will be represented is much stronger with respect to literary forms than with respect to paintings, not because authors fail to make representations that are adequate to their intentions, but because they generally do not intend their forms to be representations at all. It is for this reason that we need to be prompted to look for a representational function in the first place.[34] And since, as we have seen, the countergeneric nature of discontinuous forms is not enough to assure us that we ought to look for a representational function, we will take our cue from a certain match between indications of authorial intention on the one hand, and the resemblance between the structural configuration and the representational object on the other. The case of the open form is thus like the case of the visual representation that is not "prepackaged" as a representation: the evidence for a text's status as an open work is the same as the evidence concerning its representational meaning; hence the recognition of an open form and its interpretation are simultaneous.[35]

Unlike the art historian, however, we shall generally look for evidence of the author's intentions not in the realm of historical facts surrounding the work, but in the realm of the referential dimension of the text itself. For although the parts of an open form, when considered linguistically, reveal various techniques that serve to give the impression of discontinuity, this does not preclude the presence of a discursive argument or propositional content[36] that may provide clues to the representational meaning of the overall discontinuous structure. In this respect the verbal meaning of the text will serve a function analogous to that of the title affixed to a painting by the artist. But this more elaborate "title" may itself require elaborate interpretation, and its status as a pointer will not be established until we see the match between it and the overall structural configuration of the work. Thus the perception of a match between the discursive meaning of a text and its discontinuous structure will alert us both to the work's status as an open work and to its representational significance.

Finally, it will be noted that in abstracting from the case of the *Novum Organum* to the general procedures for interpreting open forms, I have not attached any special significance to the fact that the *Novum Organum* is a philosophical work in which the author may be seen to be speaking *in propria persona*. In short, I have been ignoring any alleged distinction between the literary and the non-literary. Although a rigorous justification of this move would require theoretical discussions that would take us beyond the scope of the present study, I might point out that even if one assumes that Bacon establishes the representational significance of the aphoristic form by speaking *in propria persona*, the very idea that a pioneering philosophical work of the Scientific Revolution has a structural configuration that is a *picture*, so to say, of its referential dimension, involves seeing the work in literary terms. Indeed, one of the aims of this study is to show that the open form not only cuts across traditional literary genres, but also bridges the gap between the "literary" and the "nonliterary." And to succeed in this task would involve contributing to the process of undermining the distinction between the literary and the nonliterary. In this respect, as in other respects, I can only hope that any procedures that I fail to justify in theoretical terms will prove to be justified by my interpretive practice.

Notes

1. *Opera Aperta: Forma e indeterminazione nella poetiche contemporanea* (Milan: Bompiani, 1962). The first chapter appeared in English as "The Poetics of the Open Work," translated by Bruce Merry, in *Twentieth Century Studies* (December 1974), and has been reprinted, in a revised version of the same translation, in Eco's *The Role of the Reader: Explorations in the Semiotics of Texts* (Bloomington: Indiana University Press, 1979), pp. 47–66. For citations from the first chapter, therefore, I shall use this revised English version. Otherwise, I shall use the French version, *L'Œuvre ouverte*, trans. Chantel Roux de Bézieux, with André Boucourechliev (Paris: Editions de Seuil, 1965), which Eco presents (p. 305) as the revision of the first Italian edition. (The second Italian edition [1967] omits large sections, with the explanation that they had meanwhile appeared separately in Italian.)

2. Umberto Eco, *The Role of the Reader*, p. 49. (*L'Œuvre ouverte*, p. 17.)

3. Ibid., p. 54. (*L'Œuvre ouverte*, p. 23.)

4. William Empson, *Seven Types of Ambiguity* (1930; reprint, New York: New Directions, 1966).

5. Ibid., p. 25.

6. *L'Œuvre ouverte*, p. 138.

7. *Role of the Reader*, p. 47. (*L'Œuvre ouverte*, p. 15.)

8. Ibid., p. 57. (*L'Œuvre ouverte*, p. 28.)

9. Ibid., p. 58. (*L'Œuvre ouverte*, p. 30.)

10. *L'Œuvre ouverte*, p. 124. Where the French edition has *nouveau*, the second Italian edition has *aperta*, which seems to make more sense in the context. Therefore my translation follows the Italian at this one point.

11. My analysis of the inconsistency between ambiguity and the signification of the whole has been implicitly based on verbal texts. Consequently, it has ignored Eco's musical paradigms. This has been done, I believe, with considerable justification. The depiction of the musician who must choose where there is no criterion for choice gives a certain force to Eco's characterization of the open work as ambiguous. The task of the interpreter is presented as interminable: condemned to construct a series of interpretations, he knows that each will come tumbling down and have to be replaced perpetually with another. Could there be more thoroughgoing ambiguity? But the application of this model to the interpretation of verbal structures (or, for that matter, to spatial structures) is quite misleading. The reader is normally not obliged to tamper with the linear order in which a text is given. Indeed, if the ordering of the elements seems arbitrary where he expects consequentiality, he

may well be impelled to seek a more consequential or coherent ordering of the elements than that given. But it is precisely such an expectation that an open text undermines. The reader will not undertake an interminable task of interpretation when it is the burden of the text to teach him that such an undertaking is pointless.

One might go so far as to argue that the Stockhausen example is misleading even with respect to music. For if the musician recognizes that her choice is completely arbitrary, then there is little likelihood that she would labor over it. She would have to choose only insofar as she has to perform the piece, but not insofar as she has to interpret it (using *interpret* in the sense of "to find the *correct* order"). If, however, she searches for the best possible arrangement of the parts, then she sees her task as that of completing the work of the composer, adding her skills to those of the composer and thus ordering the materials with which she has been presented. This would scarcely cause the musician-interpreter to see the piece as posing a question about "la possibilité d'une image unifiée et définitive de l'univers." Thus not only is Eco's musical model inapplicable to the reading of verbal works, but, equivocating as it does on the term *interpreter*, it may be misleading even with respect to music.

12. For the purposes of the present inquiry it seemed appropriate to leave out of account the question of when this recognition occurs. In fact, depending on the text and the reader, the recognition could conceivably occur at any time in the reading process or even after the text has been read through and put aside. Thus the reader could mistake an open text for an ambiguous one during a smaller or a larger portion of the reading time. It could even be that the author intended this delay in recognition to take place. Thus when one injects the phenomenology of the reading process into the discussion, there is a sense in which one could say that a work is both open and "ambiguous." This, however, is in no way inconsistent with my account, which stipulates only that as soon as the relevant data are in and the work is recognized as open, it can *no longer* be considered ambiguous. At no given moment then can a text both appear to be ambiguous and be recognized as open. Thus, although an elaboration of the temporal dimension of the reading process could perhaps enrich my account, I have no reason to suppose that it would prove to be inconsistent with it.

13. E. D. Hirsch, *Validity in Interpretation* (New Haven: Yale University Press, 1967), chap. 3.

14. For a similar notion of countergenre, although not presented with respect to the specific issues under consideration in this study, see Claudio Guillén, "On the Uses of Literary Genre," and "Genre and Countergenre: The Discovery of the Picaresque" in *Literature as System: Essays Toward the Theory of Literary History* (Princeton: Princeton University Press, 1971).

15. "Spatial Form in Modern Literature," in *The Widening Gyre: Crisis and Mastery in Modern Literature* (1963; reprint, Bloomington, Ind., 1968). An earlier version of the essay appeared in *The Sewanee Review* 53, no. 2 (1945). Although Frank has recently defended and reformulated his position, both in response to attacks against it and in the light of fashionable trends in critical theory (*Critical Inquiry* 4 [1977]: 231–52; and 5 [1978]: 275–80), my remarks are based on Frank's 1963 formulation, where the terminology is easily unpacked.

16. Ibid., p. 10.

17. Ibid., p. 16.

18. Ibid., p. 13.

19. Ibid., p. 17.

20. Ibid., p. 59.

21. Ibid., p. 28.

22. W. J. T. Mitchell notes ("Spatial Form in Literature: Toward a General Theory,"

Critical Inquiry 6 [Spring 1980]), that the spatial-form critic's distinction between spatial and linear forms embraces an unfelicitous terminology in that linearity is no less spatial than any other spatial image. Mitchell proposes substituting "tectonic" for "spatial," so as to indicate the "global, symmetrical gestalt-like image that is generally associated with spatial effects" (p. 560). This sensible suggestion, as it happens, evokes the language of the art historian Heinrich Wölfflin, whose distinction between open and closed forms in the visual arts centered on the distinction between the tectonic and the atectonic (*Principles of Art History: The Problem of the Development of Style in Later Art*, trans. M. D. Hottinger [New York: Dover, 1950], chap. 3). Although the atectonic nature of the visual open form was not characterized as linear or discontinuous, the literary counterpart of the atectonic structure would seem to be precisely the discontinuous structure to which I am applying Wölfflin's term *open form*. But just as linear forms are literally spatial, Frank's spatial form is also discontinuous; the tectonic spatial structure is recognized as underlying or transcending the discontinuity. I use *open form*, therefore, to indicate discontinuity that is supposed to be seen as discontinuity and that is not supposed to be spatialized.

23. That the italicized phrase was suppressed in the English version (*Role of the Reader*, p. 57) is perhaps attributable to the fact that this phrase accentuates the apparent incompatibility between the theory of representation that underlies the concept of the open work, and the theory of representation that Eco develops in his *Theory of Semiotics* (Bloomington: Indiana University Press, 1976), especially the critique of iconicity, pages 191–217. But even the laundered version of the theory of open work, I submit, cannot be understood independently of the concept of iconicity, independently, that is, of the notion that the open work's mode of signification is based on the resemblance between the structural configuration and certain contemporaneous ideas.

24. For a cogent and influential statement of this view, see Nelson Goodman, "Seven Strictures on Similarity," in *Problems and Projects* (Indianapolis: Bobbs-Merrill, 1972), pp. 432–47.

25. Cf. C. R. Kropf, "Unity and the Study of Eighteenth-Century Literature," *The Eighteenth Century: Theory and Interpretation* 21 (Winter 1980): 25–40. See also H. V. S. Ogden, "Variety and Contrast in Seventeenth-Century Aesthetics," *Journal of the History of Ideas* 10 (1949): 159–82.

26. Kropf, "Unity."

27. Francis Bacon, *The New Organon and Related Writings*, ed. Fulton H. Anderson (Indianapolis: Bobbs-Merrill, 1960), p. 84.

28. My analysis in chapter 2 will reveal that the form of the *Novum Organum* is not so fragmentary as Bacon's remarks on aphorisms might suggest, and that the representational significance of the work is, accordingly, more complex than is indicated by the preliminary reading recited in chapter 1.

29. E. H. Gombrich, *Art and Illusion: A Study in the Psychology of Pictorial Representation*, 2d ed. (New York: Pantheon, 1961), passim.

30. Richard Wollheim, *Art and Its Objects* (Cambridge: Cambridge University Press, 1980), pp. 205–6. For another account of visual representation that stresses the indispensability of the concept of artistic intention, see Göran Hermerén, *Representation and Meaning in the Visual Arts: A Study in the Methodology of Iconography and Iconology* (Stockholm: Läromedelsförlagen, 1969), chap. 2.

31. Wollheim, *Art and Its Objects*, pp. 206–7.

32. For such a theory of meaning, derived from Husserl's *Logische Untersuchungen*, see E. D. Hirsch, *Validity in Interpretation*.

33. My example is, of course, inspired by Picasso's juxtaposition of a bicycle saddle and handlebars in such a way as to form a representation of a bull's head. Although Picasso did

not make the bicycle, he made the representation by dint of the way he arranged the previously made elements. The handlebars were not a made resemblance until Picasso transformed them into one. In this case the authority of the artist in establishing representational meaning is analogous to that of the editor who establishes the representational meaning of the encyclopedic form (see chapter 5 below).

34. I do not mean to imply that a closed work, in which the referential aspects are neatly tied together, cannot also be seen to represent. It may be, however, that we are less likely to be consciously aware of the representational aspect of the closed form, either because it is the norm or because we are liable to be satisfied with its referential coherence and to look no further. (It may in fact be that we need deviations from the norm, namely, open forms, to make us aware of the representational aspects of closed forms.)

The notion that literary forms and genres in general represent philosophical outlooks is usually associated with the aesthetics of Hegel and his followers. Such a notion, however, was already available to Hegel—in a nonhistoricized version—in the writings of Friedrich Schlegel. In *Uber die homerische Poesie*, in *Friedrich Schlegel: Seine prosaischen Jugendschriften*, ed. J. Minor (Vienna, 1882), 1: 222–23, Schlegel distinguishes between epic and tragedy partly on the ground that the former, an indefinite mass of events, rather than a completed action, has neither a beginning nor an end, and no definite *telos (keinen bestimmten Zweck)*. In the *Geschichte der Poesie der Griechen und Römer* (Minor, 1:289), Schlegel associates the epic with contingency. Schlegel's distinctions between epic and tragedy clearly point to a notion that the two genres represent two different modes of viewing reality, one as an endless mass of contingency and the other as a purposeful whole. Hegel needed only to historicize and elaborate these distinctions, making them stages in the artistic embodiment of the progression of the Spirit.

If we look backward from Schlegel, on the other hand, we may see him as widening Aristotle's distinction between the epic and tragedy in such a way as to provide a second viable form for the imitation of reality. According to this view, Aristotle saw the correct imitation of reality as having a beginning, middle, and end, because reality is essentially teleological and has such an order. (Cf. Donald G. Marshall, "Plot as Trap, Plot as Mediation," *Bulletin of the Midwest Modern Language Association* 10 [Spring 1977]: 11–29.) Schlegel, in seeing the epic as fundamentally different from tragedy, as, in fact, the opposite of the teleological form of tragedy, sees a second possible mode of interpreting reality, namely, as contingent. According to this view of the relationship between Schlegel and Aristotle, Aristotle was the first critic to see literary form as representing a general philosophical view of reality; but since there was, for Aristotle, only one correct view of reality, there was ultimately only one correct literary form (what I would call the teleological closed form), a form that for him essentially embraced both the tragic and the epic genres. If we interpret Aristotle in this way, then the critical convention that views form as representing philosophical attitudes can be seen as providing the basis for an artistic convention as well. Thus an artist agreeing with the Aristotelian conception of reality could consciously see his use of the closed form as representing that reality, and an artist who rejected Aristotle's view of reality might devise an open form to represent his divergent philosophy.

35. As we shall see, however (in chapter 2 and in later chapters), the interpretation that presents itself simultaneously with the recognition may ultimately prove to be inadequate.

36. For an extended argument in defense of the notion that literary texts, no less than expository ones, have propositional contents, see Gerald Graff, *Poetic Statement and Critical Dogma* (Evanston, Ill.: Northwestern University Press, 1970).

2

Knowledge Broken:
Bacon's *Novum Organum*
and Diderot's *De l'Interprétation de la nature*

Thus they have directed, judg'd, conjectur'd upon, and improved *Experiments*. But lastly, in these, and all other businesses, that have come under their care; there is one thing more, about which the *Society* has been most sollicitous; and that is, the manner of their *Discourse*.
    —Thomas Sprat, *The History of the Royal Society*

Preliminary

My use of an "aspect" of the *Novum Organum* as an interpretive paradigm naturally involved a degree of simplification and, therefore, distortion. On closer inspection, for example, it will turn out that the aphoristic form of the *Novum Organum* is not so fragmentary as Bacon's remarks on aphorisms might suggest. But this fact will not force us to conclude that, in Wollheim's words, "there is no correct perception . . . nothing represented." For while the explicitly self-referential statements about the form of the work might in themselves be inadequate to the form, these statements are part of a larger pattern of verbal meaning that does match the overall discontinuous form very nicely.

This movement beyond the explicit remarks about the representational significance of the form should not seem surprising. Consider the case of a painting and its title. The title may point to a painting's representational significance without being an adequate commentary on that representational significance. Thus the relationship of adequacy is asymmetrical in that a representation may be adequate to its title without the title's being adequate to the representation. By the same token a text's statements about the

38

representational significance of its form may point to the form's status as a made resemblance without being an adequate account of its representational significance. This fact should serve to dispel any misapprehensions about the force of my previous remarks concerning the role of artistic intentions. For in subscribing to Wollheim's views on the need for a match between artistic intentions and possible perceptions, I was not imagining an intention either as an ace of spades that a critic has up his sleeve or as an ace of hearts that the artist wears on his sleeve. An intention is not a touchstone that one can adduce to validate an interpretation; it is simply the concept that underlies any judgment that a structure of evidence points to something's status as a made resemblance.

Having said this much by way of anticipation, I can move on to the main business of this chapter. Specifically, I wish to show how Bacon's views about scientific method and the structure of scientific knowledge are represented by the form of his work, and how Diderot, once he established his relationship to his mentor, was able to alter the representational significance of the aphoristic form so as to reflect his divergences from Baconian philosophy.

Aphoristic Form and "Knowledge Broken"

Diderot's *De l'Interprétation de la nature* has been called the *Novum Organum* of the eighteenth century,[1] and the filiation between the two works, at least with regard to their views on scientific method, was demonstrated by Herbert Dieckmann forty years ago.[2] Like Bacon, Diderot rejects attempts to explain nature by means of abstractions—either the abstractions of metaphysical speculation or the abstractions of mathematics. Mathematics is, in fact, "une espèce de métaphysique générale,"[3] and if metaphysics errs in its vain search after final causes and all-encompassing explanations, mathematics falsifies reality, since, in its realm, "les corps sont dépouillés de leurs qualités individuelles."[4] Like Bacon, then, Diderot is concerned with the immediate facts of experience, the harvest of observation: "Les faits, de quelque nature qu'ils soient, sont la véritable richesse du philosophe."[5] But while Diderot, like Bacon, thinks that

> la philosophie rationnelle s'occupe malheureusement beaucoup plus à rapprocher et à lier les faits qu'elle possède, qu'à en recueillir de nouveaux,[6]

rational philosophy unfortunately concerns itself more with comparing and connecting the facts that it already possesses, than with gathering new ones,

neither thinker advocates the mere gathering of facts. Rather, both
Bacon and Diderot advocate inductive methods in which the facts
yield explanations that are then verified by experiment.[7]

In view of such similarities between Diderot and Bacon with
regard to conceptions of the nature and methods of the sciences,[8] it
seems quite plausible to assume that Diderot's title, *De l'Interprétation de la nature,* derives from the subtitle of the *Novum Organum—indicia de interpretatione naturae.*

A further resemblance between Diderot's *Interprétation* and
Bacon's *Novum Organum*—a resemblance that tends to remove
any doubts about the *philosophe*'s starting point—lies in the aphoristic form of both works. And it is this resemblance with which I
am principally concerned in this chapter. Bacon saw the aphoristic
form as peculiarly suitable for the expression of his philosophical
views. More methodical or systematic literary forms, as he had
observed in *The Advancement of Learning,* "are more fit to win
consent or belief, but less fit to point to action," since they give the
impression that no further work is needed. But our knowledge of
nature is indeed fragmentary, and a fragmentary presentation, unlike a methodical one, reflects the real state of affairs and hence
induces men to pursue the Advancement of Learning:

> Aphorisms, representing a knowledge broken, do invite men to en-
> quire farther; whereas methods [i.e., systematic exposition], carrying
> the show of a total, do secure men, as if they were at furthest.[9]

And the same sort of justification of the aphoristic form is expressed in the eighty-sixth aphorism of the first book of the
Novum Organum:

> [A]dmiration of men for knowledge and arts—an admiration in itself
> weak enough and well-nigh childish—has been increased by the craft
> and artifices of those who have handled and transmitted sciences. For
> they set them forth with such ambition and parade, and bring them
> into the view of the world so fashioned and masked as if they were
> complete in all parts and finished. For if you look at the method of
> them and the divisions, they seem to embrace and comprise everything
> which can belong to the subject. And although these divisions are ill
> filled out and are but as empty cases, still to the common mind they

present the form and plan of a perfect science. But the first and most ancient seekers after truth were wont, with better faith and better fortune, too, to throw the knowledge which they gathered from the contemplation of things, and which they meant to store up for use, into aphorisms; that is, into short and scattered sentences, not linked together by an artificial method; and did not pretend or profess to embrace the entire art. But as the matter now is, it is nothing strange if men do not seek to advance in things delivered to them as long since perfect and complete.

Thus Bacon clearly sees his own use of the aphoristic form as a representation of our fragmentary knowledge of the natural order, and hence as a spur to further investigation by means of his inductive method.

Diderot, as I have already indicated, follows Bacon in the employment of the aphoristic form, and in his first aphorism, he explains his use of the form:

Je laisserai les pensées se succéder sous ma plume, dans l'ordre même selon lequel les objets se sont offerts à ma réflexion; parce qu'elles n'en représenteront que mieux les mouvements et la marche de mon esprit.[10]

I shall let my pen record my thoughts in the same order in which the objects present themselves to my reflection; thus they will better represent the changes and the progression of my mind.

This explanation, however, may sound as if it owes more to Montaigne than to Bacon. It was Montaigne, after all, who wrote in an apparently helter-skelter fashion,

Que sont-ce icy aussi, à la vérité, que crotesques et corps monstrueux, rappiecez de divers membres, sans certaine figure, n'ayants ordre, suite, ny proportion que fortuite?[11]

And what, moreover, do we have here, in truth, but grotesques, monstrous bodies patched together from various limbs, without a definite shape, lacking any order, succession, or proportion, except by chance?

and who made his *Essais* a record of his own self, of the spontaneous march of his thoughts, but whose self was equally made by his book: "Je n'ay pas plus faict mon livre que mon livre m'a faict, livre consubstantiel à son autheur. . . ."[12] But Montaigne's self-examination in the *Essais* is closely linked to a sense of the futility of examining the natural world. Following the traditional skeptical arguments, Montaigne claims that the weakness of our senses and of our rational faculties keeps us from having a certain knowledge of external reality.[13] And his retreat into the self may be seen as a "logical consequence of the view of the world as uncertain and unknowable."[14] Bacon's scientific method is in fact offered partly to overcome the skepticism that was epitomized by Montaigne. Bacon acknowledges the weakness of the senses and of the reason, but claims that an empirical method can compensate for these weaknesses:

> For the sense by itself is a thing infirm and erring; neither can instruments for enlarging or sharpening the senses do much; but all the truer kind of interpretation of nature is effected by instances and experiments fit and apposite; wherein the sense decides touching the experiment only, and the experiment touching the point in nature and the thing itself.[15]

In the light of these facts it would seem odd, at first glance, to find Diderot echoing Montaigne in a work concerned not with apprehending and examining the flux of one's thoughts, but with interpreting the external world by means of a scientific method.

But if Diderot is a Baconian to the extent that, unlike Montaigne, he is not locked in a consciousness incapable of piercing through to a knowledge of external reality, but can attain that knowledge by means of a scientific method, there is nonetheless a sense in which Diderot does bear an affinity to Montaigne. We may begin to understand this affinity, and thus the significance of Diderot's opening aphorism, by considering Diderot's conception of the role of the observer in the scientific method. For while the observer's data are not merely "subjective," their apprehension is nonetheless haphazard.[16] Diderot's observer is, in an important sense, passive with regard to the data of experience. Unlike the speculative philosopher, he does not attempt artificially to impose order on reality, but simply accepts what presents itself to him: "La philosophie expérimentale, qui ne se propose rien, est toujours contente de ce qui lui vient."[17] And this contentment is well warranted; for the experimental scientist "saisit tout ce qui lui tombe sous les mains et rencontre à la fin des choses précieuses."[18] Of course, Diderot's conception of the experimental method does not stop with the accumulation of data that fall into the hands of the scientist, but proceeds to the following stages, reflection and experimental verification; "L'observation recueille les faits; la réflex-

ion les combine; l'expérience vérifie le résultat de la combinaison."[19] It is in the light of this picture of the scientific method
that the explanation, in the opening aphorism, of the use of the
aphoristic form begins to take on its full significance. The un-
methodical order "selon lequel les objets se sont offerts à ma
réflexion" reflects the haphazard and fragmentary way in which
the data of experience present the facts of nature to the scientist's
reflective faculty—the faculty whose task it is to combine these
data and to extract explanatory hypotheses from them. Thus Diderot's use of the aphoristic form represents the fragmentary picture that nature presents even to the most conscientious observer.
But while it differs from Bacon's use of aphorisms to the extent
that it reflects our phenomenological experience of reality, whereas
Bacon's reflects the overall state of our knowledge of nature, there
is nonetheless clearly a close similarity between the intentions of
the two thinkers. Both see the aphoristic form as counteracting
claims that we already possess an orderly and complete picture of
reality.[20]

Bacon's Method and the Structure of Knowledge

Thus far I have stressed the similarity between Diderot and
Bacon with regard to their use of the aphoristic form, which, in
turn, reflects similarities between their philosophies of science.
And indeed, there would be little more to be said on this subject
were it not for the fact that the aphoristic form of Bacon's *Novum
Organum* is strikingly different from its counterpart in Diderot's
Interprétation. Although both works contain paragraphs and
sometimes groups of paragraphs that are set off and marked by
Roman numerals, Bacon's "aphorisms" are—intellectually, if not
physically—much more closely and consistently connected to one
another. If the Roman numerals and the typographical spaces between "aphorisms" in the *Novum Organum* were removed, the
work would, in fact, read to a remarkable extent like a work in
precisely that methodical or systematic form which Bacon claims
to be eschewing. Although such an assertion can be fully substan-
tiated only by recourse to the text as a whole, I can cite some
examples of the conjunctions and other palpable devices that mani-
festly link the individual "aphorisms" to those that precede them.
Consider, for example, the opening words of the following consecutive "aphorisms":

LXXIV Signs are also to be drawn from . . . ;
LXXV There is still another sign remaining . . . ;
LXXVI Neither is this other sign to be omitted . . . ;
LXXVII And as for the general opinion that . . . ;
LXXVIII I now come to the causes of these errors . . . ;
LXXIX In the second place . . . ;
LXXX To this it may be added . . . ;
LXXXI Again there is another great and powerful cause . . . ;
LXXXII And as men have misplaced the end and goal . . . ;
LXXXIII This evil, however. . . .[21]

The list could be greatly extended, but these samples suffice, I believe, to raise doubts about Bacon's "aphoristic" work as a mere assemblage of fragments.

At this point it is necessary to introduce a bit more terminological precision. I have until now—not only in this chapter, but in the previous chapter—spoken rather loosely of Bacon's "aphoristic form." Meanwhile I have suggested that literary form includes much of what has often been called "content." The physical disposition of the parts of a work is merely one of the properties that contribute to the form of the work. When Bacon speaks of aphorisms as "scattered sentences, not linked together by an artificial method," he is describing—if we understand him to be referring to an intellectual as well as to a physical scattering—an aphoristic *form*. But insofar as his aphorisms in the *Novum Organum* are "scattered" merely in the sense of being typographically distinct from one another—and this is the only scattering of which we are aware on the basis of the evidence adduced thus far—it would seem proper not to speak of them as constituting a *form*. I propose using instead the term *format*. An aphoristic *format*, the mere physical presentation of aphorisms as distinct from one another, may, of course, be part of an aphoristic *form*, but it need not be.

In Diderot's *Interprétation*, in contrast to the *Novum Organum*, although there are a half-dozen or so instances of transitions between aphorisms, there is much more an overall sense that the work consists of disconnected fragments. In fact, Herbert Dieckmann sees in the work a certain lack of intellectual coherence resulting from its fragmentation: "Because of the aphoristic and rambling character of the *Interprétation*, we do not find in it an elaborate, well-founded methodology."[22] Now having already seen that Diderot, following Bacon, consciously chose the aphoristic format as the most suitable means of expressing his views on the interpretation of nature, one is unlikely to be convinced by Dieck-mann's suggestion that any intellectual incoherence in the work results from its "rambling character." For it is the reverse relation-ship that has, I trust, already been established—namely, that the format is a representation of the lack of systematic coherence stipulated by the philosophy being presented. But Dieckmann's observation does not merely reverse the relationship between for-mat and philosophy. It points to the fact that the discontinuity of Diderot's format extends to that of his form as a whole, that the *Interprétation* manifests the aphoristic form that Bacon had de-scribed but not produced.

The question then arises: Why should the form of the *Novum Organum* consist of an aphoristic format coupled with a relatively continuous intellectual development, while the *Interprétation*—which seems to model itself both on Bacon's format and on his ideas—is much more thoroughgoing in its formal discontinuity? Is Diderot simply following his master's precept more diligently than he follows his example? And if so, why should he choose to do so? To answer these questions, we must examine more closely the ideas expressed in the works.

Bacon, as we have seen, rejects the rationalistic metaphysics of scholasticism as well as the form in which it is normally presented, since both the systematic philosophy and the systematic form give a misleadingly coherent picture of our knowledge of nature. But Bacon, of course, is not a skeptic who denies the possibility of acquiring such knowledge. Rather he sees himself as finding his way between two extremes—"between the presumption of pro-nouncing on anything and the despair of comprehending any-thing."[23] Some areas of knowledge, such as morality, are in the divine realm and beyond the scope of human investigation, but the natural world can legitimately be investigated and can effectively be understood.[24] The investigation is to be carried out by means of the author's inductive method, which will "establish progressive stages of certainty."[25]

Man properly gathers his data about nature through the senses, but the senses, in themselves, are, as we have seen, "infirm and erring." When they are harnessed by the inductive method, how-ever, they lose their infirmities. The senses, while not qualified to make judgments about nature, are qualified to "decide touching the experiment only, and the experiment [in turn decides] touching the point in nature and the thing itself."[26] Thus, through the application of an appropriate method, man is able, in an important sense, to transcend his limitations and attain a knowledge of nature.

Bacon's method is envisioned as being quite orderly. From groups of particular observations (experience) are derived general explanatory axioms, which, in turn, are verified through experiment. Although the experimental verification may require a return to particulars, the general movement of the method is upward, since the lesser axioms yield more general axioms, which, in turn, yield still more general axioms. Previous philosophy erred in speculatively jumping from particulars to the most general axioms, but Bacon's method reaches these *most* general axioms through a gradual, unbroken process:

> [B]y successive steps not interrupted or broken, we rise from particulars to lesser axioms; and then to middle axioms; and last of all to the most general.[27]

Nor, it should be stressed, does this "unbroken ascent" depend upon any special abilities possessed by practitioners of the method:

> [T]he course I propose for the discovery of sciences is such as leaves but little to the acuteness and strength of wits, but places all wits and understandings nearly on a level. For as in the drawing of a straight line or a perfect circle, much depends on the steadiness and practice of the hand, if it be done by aim of hand only, but if with the aid of rule or compass, little or nothing; so it is exactly with my plan.[28]

Finally, the primacy of method over individual intellect includes the need for the method to determine the mode of gathering and classifying the particulars on which axioms are to be based. Bacon has no sympathy with observations based on random experience, and sharply distinguishes between his method and mere accidental discovery:

> [S]imple experience . . . if taken as it comes, is called accident; if sought for, experiment. But this kind of experience is no better than a broom without its band, as the saying is—a mere groping, as of men in the dark, that feel all round for the chance of finding their way, when they had much better wait for daylight, or light a candle, and then go. But the true method of experience, on the contrary, first lights the candle, and then by means of the candle shows the way; commencing as it does with experience *duly ordered and digested, not bungling or erratic,* and

from it deducing axioms, and from established axioms again new experiments. (My italics)[29]

Thus once the method is conscientiously adopted it is, in a manner of speaking, self-sufficient. It carries mankind through a smooth, unbroken progression to a knowledge of the most general axioms concerning the natural order.

Bacon's description of his method helps to explain the formal tension that we have found in the *Novum Organum.* If the fragmentary aphoristic format represents the fragmentary state of our knowledge, and hence spurs the reader to undertake the advancement of learning, then the continuous flow from one aphorism to the next can easily be seen as the formal representation of the unbroken progress of the method that will unify all these fragmentary objects of our experience. But the continuity that opposes the aphoristic fragmentation need not be understood in terms of method alone. The picture that Bacon gives us of an unbroken ascent from particulars to more and more general axioms may be seen to represent not merely a method for acquiring knowledge, but, by implication, the ultimate structure of human knowledge itself. Each higher axiom, after all, provides a more general explanation of nature, so that the method's ascent from particular instances through more and more general axioms, is the ascent through a pyramid of explanations that reach their peak in the most general explanation of reality, the handful of axioms or the single axiom that explains all of nature. Consider in this regard the following passage from Bacon's *De Augmentis,* in which the author provides an allegorical explanation of the horns of Pan:

> Horns are attributed to the Universe, broad at the base and pointed at the top. For all nature rises to a point like a pyramid. Individuals, which lie at the base of nature, are infinite in number; these are collected into Species, which are themselves manifold; the Species rise again into Genera; which also by continual gradations are contracted into more universal generalities, so that at last nature seems to end as it were in unity; as is signified by the pyramidal form of the horns of Pan.[30]

The pyramid thus is Bacon's image of the natural universe, and the "unbroken" method that Bacon describes in the *Novum Organum* carries us from the base of the pyramid to its apex. The continuity of Bacon's method thus parallels the unified structure of our potential knowledge, which in turn will reflect the unified structure of the natural order.[31] The continuity then, which combats the apparently fragmentary form of the *Novum Organum*, opposes to the present state of knowledge not only a unified method, but the unified knowledge of reality that the method will provide.

Science *en tâtonnant* and the Search for General Explanations

Diderot, as we have seen, patterns his method in the *Interprétation* on Bacon's method. Where Bacon speaks of experience, then axioms, then experiments, Diderot speaks of "l'observation de la nature, la réflexion, et l'expérience." Where then does Diderot's method differ from Bacon's in such a way as to account for the more thoroughgoing fragmentation of the *Interprétation*'s aphoristic form?

One significant point of difference between Diderot and Bacon centers on the role of the investigator's intellect in scientific method.[32] Bacon's description of the "unbrokenness" of his method and his insistence that special ability was not required have helped to give readers the impression that, as Whitehead put it, "he had in his mind the belief that with a sufficient care in the collection of instances the general law would stand out of itself."[33] Modern philosophy of science, on the other hand, tends to see the emergence of the general law, that is, Bacon's axiom, not as following automatically from a proper method, but as requiring a special intellectual effort on the part of the scientist. What is required is the framing of a hypothesis, which arises, not from the facts themselves, but from the ability of the investigator. "The framing of hypotheses," according to Bertrand Russell, "is the more difficult part of scientific work, and the part where great ability is indispensable. So far, no method has been found which would make it possible to invent hypotheses by rule."[34] Such considerations have resulted in the frequent criticism of Bacon for his underestimation of the role of hypotheses in scientific inquiry.[35]

Bacon's overestimation of the power of the methodical rules thus involves an underestimation of the role of the individual intellect in scientific discovery. Diderot, on the other hand, while not formulating a modern description of the role of hypothesis, does tend, at various points in the *Interprétation*, to recognize the role of individual ability, and, in fact, of scientific genius. And, as the importance of the individual rises, the self-sufficiency of the method becomes less pronounced. It will be recalled that Diderot stresses that "les faits, de quelque nature qu'ils soient, sont la véritable richesse du philosophe." In doing so he tends to ignore Bacon's distinction between "bungling and erratic experience," on the one hand, and experience that is "duly ordered and digested," on the other. The erratic sort of simple experience, as we have seen, is rejected by Bacon as "mere groping." But Diderot makes a virtue of groping:

> [La philosophie expérimentale] a les yeux bandés, marche toujours en tâtonnant, saisit tout ce qui lui tombe sous les mains, et rencontre à la fin des choses précieuses.[36]

> [Experimental philosophy] is blindfolded and always gropes as it goes, seizing everything that it comes across; and in the end, it encounters precious things.

It is not that random facts speak for themselves, but that certain observers may extract profound truths from them. One class of observer that Diderot cites is that of the "manœuvriers d'opérations les plus grossiers," whose "grande habitude de faire des expériences" gives them "un pressentiment qui a le caractère de l'inspiration." The "inspiration," of course, is something quite distinct from mere method. It is akin to the "sentiment" by which "gens de goût jugent des ouvrages d'esprit." The "grands manœuvriers" may serve science by passing on to others not so much their procedures as their insightfulness:

> Ainsi le service le plus important qu'ils aient à rendre à ceux qu'ils initient à la philosophie expérimentale, c'est bien moins de les instruire du procédé et du résultat, que de faire passer en eux cet esprit de divination par lequel on *subodore*, pour ainsi dire, des procédés inconnus, des expériences nouvelles, des résultats ignorés.[37]

> Thus the most important service that they can render to those whom they initiate into experimental philosophy is less to instruct them in methods and results than to transmit to them the spirit of inspired guesswork, with which one can, so to speak, "sniff out" new experiments, unknown methods and results.

Diderot, in introducing the insights of the individual, is not abandoning Bacon's notion of method, but is certainly depriving it of its primacy. Method is not the only dependable source of knowledge, to be effectively used no matter what the intellectual ability of the practitioner, but it becomes for Diderot something of a consolation for those who wish to be scientists but lack genius:

> Ouvrez l'ouvrage de Franklin, feuilletez les livres des chimistes, et vous verrez combien l'art expérimental exige de vues, d'imagination, de sagacité, de ressources: lisez-les attentivement, parce que s'il est possible d'apprendre en combien de manières une expérience se retourne, c'est là que vous l'apprendrez. Si, au défaut de génie, vous avez besoin d'un moyen technique qui vous dirige, ayez sous les yeux une table des qualités, qu'on a reconnues jusqu'à présent dans la matière, [etc.].[38]

> Open Franklin's book, leaf through the works of the chemists, and you will see how much the experimental method requires vision, imagination, sagacity, resourcefulness: read them attentively, for if it is possible to learn in how many ways one can get results from an experiment, it is there that you will learn it. If, lacking genius, you need a technique to guide you, then turn to a table of the properties that have been found in a substance [etc.].

If the primacy and continuity of Bacon's method, as described in the *Novum Organum,* are represented by the continuity of the aphorisms, I think it is now easy to see how Diderot's exaltation of random groping and scientific genius gives science a more haphazard and irregular—and less predictable—quality, such as is represented by the discontinuities between the aphorisms of the *Interprétation.*

But there still remains the question of the ultimate structure of knowledge. Is there no counterpart in Diderot of Bacon's pyramid of knowledge? Does Diderot not envision a general unifying axiom that scientific genius will ultimately grasp?

In the important but confusing Aphorism XLV, Diderot states that just as the properties of a curve turn out to be different aspects of the same property, experimental science will one day show us that all phenomena, whether of elasticity, attraction, magnetism, or electricity, are "faces différentes de la même affection." Thus he seems to be saying that science will reveal a coherent structure of nature. But he then goes on to question whether the central phenomenon that could reveal this unified structure exists at all, and in so doing he seems to undermine the notion that there is a unified structure of scientific knowledge:

> Mais au défaut de ce centre de correspondance commune, ils [the known phenomena] demeureront isolés; toutes les découvertes de la

physique expérimentale ne feront que les rapprocher en s'interposant, sans jamais les réunir, et quand elles parviendraient à les réunir, elles en formeraient un cercle continu de phénomènes où l'on ne pourrait discerner quel serait le premier et quel serait le dernier. Ce cas singulier, où la physique expérimentale, à force de travail, aurait formé un labyrinthe dans lequel la physique rationnelle, égarée et perdue, tournerait sans cesse, n'est pas impossible dans la nature, comme il l'est en mathématiques.[39]

But in the absence of this locus of connections, they [the known phenomena] will remain isolated; all the discoveries of experimental physics will do no more than reduce the distance between them, without ever tying them together; and even if the discoveries should succeed in tying the phenomena together, they would form a continuous circle where it would be impossible to determine which phenomenon was the first and which the last. This singular situation, in which experimental physics, by dint of its own labors, would have constructed a labyrinth in which rational physics, bewildered and lost, would spin endlessly, is not impossible in nature, as it is in mathematics.

Diderot's "phénomène central" corresponds to the apex of Bacon's pyramid. But unlike Bacon's most central axiom, Diderot's "phénomène central" need not exist. And even if it should, its discovery is not a necessary consequence of the application of the experimental method. Without the doubtful "phénomène central," the phenomena of nature will remain isolated, or, at best, linked in a circle in which the relationship between the parts remains obscure. Finally, then, we are left with the possibility that experimental science will lead us into a labyrinth in which the rational branch of science, that responsible for ordering the phenomena, for making ultimate sense of the data, will find itself bewildered and lost, spinning endlessly.

We saw earlier that, while embracing a scientific method that vanquishes the skeptic's view of consciousness as a sort of prison from which the senses and reason offer no escape, Diderot retained, in that scientific method itself, the Montaignean notion that consciousness is something of a passive recipient of haphazard (albeit in this case veridical) images. But now we can see that Montaigne's skepticism itself is not altogether absent in Diderot's conception of science. For although Diderot does not put into question the scientist's ability to achieve dependable knowledge of the external world, he does question the amenability of the external world to ultimate explanation. It is as if Diderot has taken the skepticism that Montaigne and others had interposed between consciousness and the world, and projected it onto the world itself.[40]

Bacon urged an inductive method instead of the deductive method of mathematics, but the results of his method, like those of mathematics, would be unified, structured, certain, and inevitable. Diderot believes that science, unlike mathematics, may lead us into a hopeless labyrinth. He thus offers neither a smooth and autonomous method, nor the prospect of the inevitable results of such a method, namely, a unified picture of reality. There is, consequently, no strong unifying principle in Diderot's *Interprétation* to offset the fragmenting effect of the random collection of observations; there is no power that can pull together the aphorisms and make them a unified whole.

Notes

1. Arthur M. Wilson, *Diderot* (New York: Oxford University Press, 1972), pp. 187–88.
2. Herbert Dieckmann, "The Influence of Francis Bacon on Diderot's *Interprétation de la Nature*," *Romanic Review* 34 (1943): 303–29.
3. *De l'Interprétation de la nature*, in Denis Diderot, *Œuvres philosophiques*, ed. Paul Vernière (Paris: Garnier, n.d.), #II. In this and subsequent references to the *Interprétation*, the roman numeral refers to the number of the aphorism cited.
4. Ibid.
5. Ibid., #XX.
6. Ibid.
7. The fact that Bacon and Diderot hold such similar views raises an interesting historical question. Bacon voiced his suspicions of mathematics before Newton and others had definitively established it as an invaluable tool of science. Diderot wrote the *Interprétation* (1753) more than sixty years after the publication of Newton's *Principia*, and well after Newton's apotheosis as a deity of the Enlightenment. Why then should Diderot offer such seemingly anachronistic views? For an answer, see Ernst Cassirer's suggestive remarks in the second chapter (especially pp. 74–80) of *The Philosophy of the Enlightenment* (Boston: Beacon Press, 1955). Cassirer likens Diderot's rejection of mathematics because of its faulty descriptive powers to the Newtonians' rejection of Descartes on the same grounds. He also points to Buffon's nominalistic rejection of Linnaeus's system of classification as a model for Diderot's nonmathematical method. Cf. Dieckmann, "The Influence of Francis Bacon," pp. 307–9.
8. The substantive scientific problems about which Diderot offers conjectures in the last part of the *Interprétation* reflect his concern with the contemporary issue of the materialistic explanation of biological phenomena, including consciousness, while Bacon's examples in the *Novum Organum* have largely to do with heat and its explanation in terms of molecular motion. But these substantive, as opposed to methodological or epistemological, issues lie outside the concerns of this study.
9. Francis Bacon, *Works,* ed. Spedding, Ellis, and Heath (Boston, 1861–64), 6:292.
10. *De l'Interprétation de la nature*, #I.

11. Michel de Montaigne, *Essais* (Paris: Garnier, 1962), 1: 198 (bk. 1, chap. 28).

12. Ibid., 2: 69 (bk. 2, chap. 18).

13. Cf. Richard H. Popkin, *The History of Scepticism from Erasmus to Spinoza* (Berkeley: University of California Press, 1979), chap. 3.

14. R. A. Sayce, *The Essays of Montaigne: A Critical Exploration* (London: Weidenfeld and Nicholson, 1972), p. 320.

15. Francis Bacon, *New Organon and Related Writings*, ed. Fulton H. Anderson (Indianapolis: Bobbs-Merrill, 1960), I, #L. In this and subsequent references to the *Novum Organum*—except for references to the author's preface, which will be indicated by page number—the first Roman numeral refers to the book number, and the second Roman numeral refers to the number of the aphorism.

16. For a view of the relationship between Montaigne and Diderot's *Interprétation* that differs substantially from the one offered here, see Jerome Schwartz, *Diderot and Montaigne: The Essais and the Shaping of Diderot's Humanism* (Geneva: Droz, 1966), pp. 75–79.

17. *De l'Interprétation de la nature*, #XXV.

18. Ibid., #XXIII.

19. Ibid., #XV.

20. Cf. Wilson, *Diderot*, p. 191.

21. These transitions are no less conspicuous in the Latin original: LXXIV Capienda etiam sunt signa ex incrementis. . . ; LXXV Etiam aliud signum capiendum est. . . ; LXXVI Neque illud signum praetermittendum est. . . ; LXXVII Quod vero putant homines. . . ; LXXVIII Jam vero veniendum ad causas errorum. . . ; LXXIX At secundo loco. . . ; LXXX Accedit et illud. . . ; LXXXI Rursus se ostendit alia causa potens. . . ; LXXXII Quemadmodum autem finis et meta scientiarum male posita sunt apud homines. . . ; LXXXIII Excrevit autem mirum in modum istud malum. . . ; *Works*, 1 :280–90.

22. Dieckmann, "The Influence of Francis Bacon," p. 303.

23. *New Organon*, author's preface, p. 33.

24. *The Great Instauration*, in *New Organon*, p. 15.

25. *New Organon*, author's preface, p. 33.

26. Ibid., I, #I.

27. Ibid., I, #CIV. Cf. I, #XIX.

28. Ibid., I, #LXI.

29. Ibid., I, #LXXXII.

30. *De dignitate et augmentis scientiarum*, in *Works*, 8 :449.

31. Cf. Robert McRae, "The Unity of the Sciences: Bacon, Descartes, and Leibniz," *Journal of the History of Ideas* 8 (January 1957): 29–30.

32. For a substantive comparison to which I am indebted at several points in the following paragraphs, see Dieckmann, "The Influence of Francis Bacon."

33. Alfred North Whitehead, *Science and the Modern World* (1925; reprint, New York: Mentor, 1948), p. 44.

34. Bertrand Russell, *A History of Western Philosophy* (1948; reprint, New York: Simon and Schuster, 1964), pp. 544–45.

35. See, for example, Karl Popper, *The Logic of Scientific Discovery* (New York: Basic Books, 1959), pp. 279–80: "It is possible to interpret the ways of science more prosaically. One might say that progress can . . . 'come about only in two ways: by gathering new perceptual experiences, and by better organizing those which are available already.' But this description of scientific progress, although not actually wrong, seems to miss the point. It is too reminiscent of Bacon's induction; too suggestive of his industrious gathering of the 'countless grapes, ripe and in season,' from which he expected the wine of science to flow:

of his myth of a scientific method that starts from observation and experiment and then proceeds to theories. . . . Out of interpreted sense-experiences science cannot be distilled, no matter how industriously we gather and sort them. Bold ideas, unjustified anticipations, and speculative thought, are our only means for interpreting nature: our only organon, our only instrument for grasping her."

In recent years, however, some scholars have attempted to defend Bacon from the charge that his method lacked the modern notion of hypothesis as a bold leap beyond the observations. See, for example, Peter Caw's article "Scientific Method" in the *Encyclopedia of Philosophy* vol. 7; Mary Horton, "In Defence of Francis Bacon: A Criticism of the Critics of the Inductive Method," in *Studies in the History and Philosophy of Science* 4 (1973): 241–78; and Curt J. Ducasse, "Francis Bacon's Philosophy of Science," in *Theories of Scientific Method: The Renaissance Through the Nineteenth Century,* ed. Edward H. Madden (Seattle: University of Washington Press, 1960), pp. 50–74. These defenses tend to be based on reinterpretations of what Bacon meant or had to have meant by such terms as *anticipation, experiment, first vintage, means of order.* Whatever merits the various arguments may have—and they cannot be evaluated here—they fail to account for Bacon's insistence, in the *Novum Organum,* that his method will yield a consistent, "unbroken" rise to more and more general axioms, and that science does not require special abilities. Neither of these points seems consistent with modern notions of the role of hypothesis in scientific method. For if hypotheses do not simply emerge from the collected observations, and if they require a bold act of speculation, then they are not going to be produced by mediocre minds whose abilities are enhanced by the instrument of method, and they are not going to emerge in a predictable, unbroken sequence. It is Bacon's clearly expressed confidence in the virtues of the method, as opposed to those of its practitioners, and in the relentless smoothness of its results, on which my interpretation of the form of the *Novum Organum* finally rests.

36. *De l'Interprétation de la nature,* #XXIII.

37. Ibid., #XXX.

38. Ibid., #XLI.

39. Ibid., #XLV.

40. It should be noted that in characterizing Diderot's position as *skeptical* I am, for the sake of the comparison with Montaigne, using the term rather loosely. Since I try to make it clear, however, just what I mean by a "skepticism" that "is projected . . . onto the world itself," I trust that my usage is in no way misleading. Technically speaking, skepticism is an epistemological position that asserts, in the manner of Montaigne, that knowledge is unattainable and doubt therefore necessary. However, it has been observed that since classical Pyrrhonism based its doctrine of doubt on the "equivalence des raisons contraires" (V. Brochard, *Les Sceptiques grecs* [Paris: J. Vrin, 1959], p. 57), it may be seen as a certain kind of metaphysical dogmatism, one that asserts that there exists an equal number of arguments, and hence an equal amount of evidence in the universe for and against every proposition (Stephen Pepper, *World Hypotheses: A Study in Evidence* [Berkeley: University of California Press, 1942], pp. 6–7). Diderot's skepticism is also metaphysical, but in a different way. In claiming that there need be no "phénomène central," Diderot is pointing toward a view according to which the phenomena of nature may be essentially discrete individuals that do not form themselves into any ontological or explanatory hierarchy. This view recurs in Diderot's article "Encyclopédie": "L'univers ne nous offre que des êtres particuliers, infinis en nombre, et sans presque aucune division fixe et déterminée; il n'y en a aucun qu'on puisse appeler le premier ou le dernier" (Denis Diderot, *Œuvres complètes,* ed. J. Assezat [Paris, 1876], vol. 14, p. 451). Diderot's "skepticism," then, is really a form of nominalism. (The relationship between Diderot's nominalism and the form of the *Encyclopédie* will be examined in chapter 5.)

3

Perspectivism and Inclusionism:
The Case of the *Quijote*

Quelle bonté est-ce que je voyois hyer en credit, et demain
plus, et que le traict d'une rivière faict crime?
Quelle verité que ces montaignes bornent, qui est mensonge
au monde qui se tient au delà?
—Michel de Montaigne, *Apologie de Raimond Sebond*

Preliminary

Bacon's remarks about aphorisms, along with Diderot's and
Montaigne's remarks about the forms of their works, should have
the effect of allaying any suspicions that this is one of those studies
which set out to interpret older texts in ways that would have
amazed or befuddled their authors. Nonetheless, we have seen that
an adequate interpretation of the open forms of Bacon and Diderot
required that we move from the authors' explicit remarks about the
forms of their works to more comprehensive interpretations of
their texts.

In the *Quijote* we have, I shall argue, another work whose discontinuous form represents an epistemological viewpoint, in this
case, value skepticism. And, again, we have remarks about the
form of the work which, before they can yield an interpretation of
the novel's digressive form, need to be related to a larger structure
of meaning. In this way, the *Quijote,* like the aphoristic works just
discussed, manifests a homology between its propositional content
and its discontinuity. In one important respect, however, the *Quijote* goes beyond the *Novum Organum* and *L'Interprétation.* For
its reflexivity does not merely point to its digressive form as an
extra dimension of meaning, a "picture" of its propositional content, but explains the indispensability of that form. Specifically,

once we understand the aesthetic, ethical, and epistemological propositions that are operating in the novel, we can understand how the work's digressive structure does not merely represent the content of those propositions, but is dictated by them.

It will be convenient to begin our survey of the philosophical postulates enunciated in the *Quijote* by contrasting the work's pronouncements on aesthetics with more recent and more familiar views on the subject, namely, those of Henry James.

Truth and Digression

The task of the novelist, according to James, is to circumscribe a subject, to treat a dependent part of reality as if it were an independent whole:

> Really universally, relations stop nowhere, and the exquisite problem of the artist is eternally but to draw by a geometry of his own, the circle within which they shall happily *appear* to do so.[1]

For James, art has a symmetry, a completeness that life lacks. While real relations stretch on and on, there is a value, that of the polished, closed work of art, which demands the exclusion of the *apparently* extraneous. This exclusion then is no longer arbitrary; for while the endless expanse of interrelations allows for no real priority to any one segment, aesthetic values dictate the shape to be taken by the representation of reality. The facts relating to the life of an individual cannot be disentangled from an endless array of facts; nor can they lay claim to a greater importance or greater value than other chains of facts. But a work of art achieves value by arranging a group of facts and artfully cutting them off from all further entanglements. Thus the form of a literary work is dictated by the value of form.

In accordance with this formalistic view the violation of the closed circle of a work of art would result from the inclusion of that which does not *appear* indispensable to the subject at hand. The artist must find the boundaries of indispensability. "Where," he must ask "for the complete expression of one's subject, does a particular relation stop—giving way to some other not concerned in that expression?"[2]

Before the advent of James, and the formalists who relied on him, the chief criterion of literary value was often that of truth.

And this is the criterion to which the *Quijote* repeatedly adverts. Not that everything in a literary work should be factually true; but the work as a whole functioned to present truths, particularly moral truths, and its parts or details were expected to contribute to that function. In the context of this classical attitude toward literature, the terms *relevance* and *pertinence* seem appropriate substitutes for James's more rigorous *indispensability.* To be relevant a part of a literary work should contribute to the truth being presented. That which departs from or interrupts the presentation of truth is irrelevant. The doctrine is often voiced in the *Quijote,* where irrelevancies, or "digressions," as they are called in the book, are repeatedly condemned. For example, when we are presented with Don Quijote's arrival at the house of the Caballero del Verde Gabán, we learn that the translator has seen fit to omit Cide Hamete's descriptions of the place:

> Aquí pinta el autor todas las circunstancias de la casa de don Diego, pintándonos en ellas lo que contiene una casa de un caballero labrador y rico; pero al traductor desta historia le pareció pasar estas y otras semejantes menudencias en silencio, porque no venían bien con el propósito principal de la historia; la cual más tiene su fuerza en la verdad que en las frías digresiones.[3]

> Here the author paints all the details of Don Diego's home, describing the contents of a rich gentleman farmer's house. But it seems right to the translator of this history to pass over these and other such particulars in silence, for they do not suit the principal purpose of this history, which derives its strength rather from truth than from sterile digressions. (P. 580)[4]

Later Don Quijote himself reproaches the boy-narrator of the puppet show for including a single digressive clause in his narration, again on the ground that details should support the truth toward which the narrative is pointing:

> "Niño, niño," dijo con voz alta a esta sazón don Quijote, "seguid vuestra historia línea recta, y no os metáis en las curvas o transversales; que para sacar una verdad en limpio menester son muchas pruebas y repruebas." (II, xxvi, 731)

> "Boy, boy," said Don Quijote at this point, in a loud voice, "go straight ahead with your story, and do not go curving off at a tangent; for it requires much proof and corroboration to bring a truth to the light." (Pp. 639–40)

Such pronouncements, urging relevance to the truth as the criterion of inclusion, and rejecting as digressive any detail that does not serve "para sacar una verdad en limpio," will strike readers of the *Quijote* as paradoxical, since the book as a whole reads like a fabric of digressions, ranging from apparently arbitrary details to long interpolated narratives. In fact, this element of paradox is accentuated by the technique of linking the condemnation of digression with the commission of it. For example, the passage eschewing detailed description of Don Diego's house is followed immediately by an uncharacteristically detailed description of Don Quijote's costume and other items including the water with which he cleansed himself:

> Entraron a don Quijote en una sala, desarmóle Sancho, quedó en valones y en jubón de camuza, todo bisunto con la mugre de las armas: el cuello era valona a lo estudiantil, sin almidón y sin randas; los borceguíes eran datilados, y encerados los zapatos. Ciñóse su buena espada, que pendía de un tahalí de lobos marinos; que es opinión que muchos años fué enfermo de los riñones; cubrióse un herreruelo de buen paño pardo; pero antes de todo con cinco calderos, o seis, de agua, que en la cantidad de los calderos hay alguna diferencia, se lavó la cabeza y rostro, y todavía se quedó el agua de color de suero, merced a la golosina de Sancho y a la compra de sus negros requesones, que tan blanco pusieron a su amo. (II, xviii, 662–63)

> They led Don Quixote into a hall, where Sancho took off his armour, leaving him in his Walloon breeches and chamois leather jerkin, all stained with the grime of his armour. He wore a Vandyke collar like a student's, unstarched and without lace, date-coloured leggings and waxed shoes. He carried his good sword slung over his shoulders on a sealskin strap, he having, it is believed, a long-standing weakness of the kidneys; and over all this he wore a cloak of good grey cloth. But first of all he had washed his face and head with five or six buckets of water—there is some difference of opinion as to the number—the water remaining always the colour of whey, thanks to Sancho's gluttony and his purchase of those foul curds that turned his master so fair. (Pp. 580–81)

By the same token Don Quijote's injunction to the boy-narrator may be seen to be more digressive than the digression that it is attacking.

Variations on this pattern occur several more times in the *Quijote*. For example, when Don Quijote is relating what he saw in the cueva de Montesinos, he is interrupted by Sancho, who speculates on the manufacture of the dagger with which Montesinos had cut out the heart of his friend Durandarte:

> "Debía de ser . . . el tal puñal de Ramón de Hoces, el Sevillano." (II, xxiii, 704)

> "That must be . . . the dagger made by Ramon de Hoces of Seville." (P. 616)

His master replies as follows:

> "No sé . . . pero no sería dese puñalero porque Ramón de Hoces fué ayer, y lo de Roncesvalles, donde aconteció esta desgracia, ha muchos años, y esta averiguación no es de importancia, ni turba ni altera la verdad y contesto de la historia." (II, xxiii, 704)

> "I do not know. . . . But it could not be that dagger-maker, because Ramon de Hoces was living yesterday, and the fight at Roncesvalles, where this tragedy occurred, was many years ago. But inquiry into that is of no importance, for it does not disturb or alter the truth and sequence of the history." (P. 616)

Here Don Quijote cannot refrain from digressively considering the merits of the question before dismissing it as digressive. A similar pattern is repeated a few pages later, except that here it is Sancho, who, after disputing his master's contention that the man who had told them about the *aventura del rebuzno* must have been mistaken in identifying the *rebuznadores* as *regidores* rather than as *alcaldes*, rejects the problem as irrelevant:

> "Señor, en eso no hay que reparar; que bien puede ser que los regidores que entonces rebuznaron viniesen con el tiempo a ser alcaldes de su pueblo, y así, se pueden llamar con entrambos títulos; cuanto más que no hace al caso a la verdad de la historia ser los rebuznadores alcaldes o regidores, como ellos una por una hayan rebuznado; porque tan a pique está de rebuznar un alcalde como un regidor." (III, xxvii, 740–41)

> "There's nothing in that, sir. It's perfectly possible that the aldermen who brayed have come in course of time to be bailiffs of their village, and so they can be called by either title. What's more, it doesn't affect the truth of the story whether the brayers were bailiffs or aldermen, since they brayed anyway; for a bailiff's as good a brayer as an alderman." (P. 648)

Here both Don Quijote's comment and Sancho's response form a digression in Cide Hamete's description of the confrontation that the two are witnessing. Sancho thus cannot reject the irrelevancy without adding to it.

These digressive rejections of digression exhibit a playful use of paradox that Cervantes shared with Erasmus, Rabelais, and other Renaissance writers.[5] And in view of the fact that the playful passages that I have cited all occur in the second part, it is reasonable to suppose that this paradoxical digressiveness is a response to criticisms of the digressiveness—particularly in the matter of interpolated narratives—of the first part. One response to such criticism, we are told (II, xliv, 848–49), has been Cide Hamete's omission, in the second part, of long interpolated narratives, and his relatively sparing use even of shorter digressive tales. But the inclusion of the playful digressions that we have been considering demonstrates that neither Cide Hamete nor Cervantes was sufficiently chastened by criticism to renounce digressions altogether.

It was once common to view early novelists and their precursors as undisciplined primitives who lacked any conception of their genre's potential for artistic maturity. According to such a view, a digressive novelist was digressive because he did not know any better, because he lacked James's insight into the superiority of circumscribed art over unwieldy reality. Yet the digressiveness of the *Quijote*, as we have already seen, was not naive, and if the book is not rejecting formalism before the fact, its conscious and multifarious use of digressions is surely intended to do something more than taunt captious readers. The form of the book is, of course, a function of its digressiveness. This digressiveness, as we shall see, involves not only narrative inconsequentiality but also stylistic and generic heterogeneity. These features, in turn, reflect intellectual and imaginative processes, and it is in terms of these that the form is ultimately to be understood.

Perspectivism

A celebrated aspect of the *Quijote* is its so-called perspectivism. Things are continually seen from more than one point of view. In questions of fact, the narrator generally tells us which perspective is the accurate one.[6] Thus we are not left in doubt about whether a given object is a giant, as Don Quijote claims, or a windmill, as Sancho claims; Mambrino's helmet, as Don Quijote claims, or a barber's basin, as Sancho and the barber claim. But when perspectives differ with regard to value, the narrator is not nearly so helpful. In the tale of El Cautivo, for example, there is a central moral ambiguity. Is Zoraida to be praised for embracing Christianity or condemned for betraying her father? The narrator never tells us. Nor is the moral perspectivism in the episode merely implicit. Consider, for example, the Cautivo's description of the promontory where Zoraida's father and the other Moors are to be put ashore:

> un pequeño promontorio o cabo que de los moros es llamado el de *la Caba Rumía*, que en nuestra lengua quiere decir *la mala mujer cristiana;* y es tradición entre los moros que en aquel lugar está enterrada la Cava, por quien se perdió España. . . ; y aun tienen por mal agüero llegar allí a dar fondo cuando la necesidad les fuerza a ello, porque nunca le dan sin ella; puerto que para nostros no fue abrigo de mala mujer, sino puerto seguro de nuestro remedio, según andaba alterada la mar. (I, xli, 426)

> a small promontory or cape, which is called by the Moors the Cape of the *"Cava Rumia";* which means in our language the wicked Christian woman. For there is a tradition among the Moors that it is the place where that *"Cava"* lies buried, through whom Spain was lost; for *"cava"* in their tongue means wicked woman and *"rumia"* Christian. They even look on it as a bad omen to have to anchor there, if necessity drives them to—and otherwise they never do so. But for us it was no wicked woman's shelter, but a secure haven of refuge, as the sea was running high. (P. 374)

Here the clash of perspectives is presented quite explicitly and Cide Hamete is unwilling and probably unable to settle the issue for us. He is, after all, a Moor, and his personal perspective would presumably oppose that of the Cautivo: he would find the cape of the Caba Rumía to be a wicked place. But this judgment, unlike the judgment about windmills, could scarcely be definitive. Even the vigilant and resourceful Cide Hamete cannot determine absolutely whether the cape is a good or an evil place.

Such moral perspectivism is repeated a few paragraphs later, when Zoraida justifies herself to her wretched father:

> "Alá sabe bien que no pude hacer otra cosa de la que he hecho, y que estos cristianos no deben nada a mi voluntad, pues aunque quisiera no venir con ellos y quedarme en mi casa, me fuera imposible, según la priesa que me daba mi alma a poner por obra *ésta que a mi me parece*

tan buena como tú, padre amado, la juzgas por mala." (I, xli, 427; italics mine)

"Allah well knows that I could have done nothing but what I did, and that these Christians owe me nothing for my goodwill. For even if I had wanted not to come with them, but to stay at home, it would have been impossible. So fast did my soul hurry me towards *a deed which appears as good to me, beloved father, as it appears wicked to you.*" (P. 375)

Elsewhere the opposing moral perspectives are to be found in a single character, so as to cloud our judgment of him. For example, after Sanson Carrasco, disguised as the Caballero de la Blanca Luna, has finally vanquished Don Quijote, he explains that he had persevered in his project, despite his painful defeat as the Caballero de los Espejos, in order to restore the misguided knight to his senses. He asks that his identity not be revealed

"porque tengan efecto los buenos pensamientos míos y vuelva a cobrar su juicio un hombre que le tiene bonísimo." (II, lxv, 1014)

"so that my good plan may work, and his understanding be restored to him; for he has an excellent brain." (P. 892)

The reader by now may question whether "restoring Don Quijote to his senses" is the best possible course, but in addition he has grounds to question Carrasco's motives. After his earlier defeat at the hands of Don Quijote, Carrasco had declared:

"pensar que yo he de volver a la [casa] mía hasta haber molido a palos a don Quijote es pensar en lo escusado; y no me llevará ahora a buscarle el deseo de que cobre su juicio, sino el de la venganza; que el dolor grande de mis costillas no me deja hacer más piadosos discursos." (II, xv, 642)

"but it would be folly to suppose that I shall go back home till I have thrashed Don Quixote. And it will not be the desire to restore him to his senses that will drive me after him, but the desire for revenge; for the pain in my ribs will not allow me to make more charitable speeches." (P. 561)

It is, of course, "piadosos discursos" that Carrasco delivers to Don Antonio, and if the private admission of vindictiveness just quoted had been juxtaposed with the pious pronouncements of the Caballero de la Blanca Luna, it would be easy to condemn Carrasco for a hypocrite. But his angry vindictiveness had been expressed long before, and had perhaps reflected merely the heat of the moment. His anger may have passed and his motives may now be sincere. We do not know whether they are or not. Moreover, it is likely that Carrasco himself does not know.

A third sort of moral perspectivism occurs when the first narrator, Cide Hamete, prompts the reader to make a judgment that the reader later comes to question. A prime example is Cide Hamete's attitude toward the "grave eclesiástico" of the Duke and Duchess. He is initially presented in quite unfavorable terms:

> La duquesa y el duque salieron a la puerta de la sala. . . , y con ellos un grave eclesiástico destos que gobiernan las casas de los príncipes; destos que como no nacen príncipes, no aciertan a enseñar cómo lo han de ser los que lo son; destos que quieren que la grandeza de los grandes se mida con la estrecheza de sus ánimos; destos que, queriendo mostrar a los que ellos gobiernan a ser limitados, les hacen ser miserables; destos tales, digo, que debía de ser el grave religioso. (II, xxxi, 765)

> The Duke and Duchess came to the door of the hall to receive him, and with them one of those grave ecclesiastics who rule the houses of princes; of those who, not being born princes themselves, do not succeed in teaching those who are how to behave as such; who would have the greatness of the great measured by the narrowness of their own souls; who, wanting to show those they rule how to be frugal, make them miserly; such a man, I mean, was this grave ecclesiastic. (P. 670)

Consequently, when such a man goes on to reproach the Duke for humoring Don Quijote (II, xxxi, 768), the reader sees this censoriousness as the natural expression of the dour "estrecheza de sus ánimos," the "narrowness of his soul." As the tricks played on the knight errant begin to pile up, however, the reader is likely to become increasingly disenchanted with the Duke and Duchess, to find them to be idle and cruel. Cide Hamete himself, while relating later episodes, makes veiled comments on their behavior. For example, after stating that Don Antonio Moreno sought for "modos como, sin su perjuicio, sacase a plaza sus [Don Quijote's] locuras," for "ways of bringing Don Quijote's madness into view without harming him," the narrator says, presumably contrasting Don Antonio with the Duke and Duchess, "porque no son burlas las que duelen," "because jests that cause injury are no jests" (II, lxii, 988).

More explicitly, a few chapters later, we are finally told that Cide Hamete says

> que tiene para sí ser tan locos los burladores como los burlados, y que no estaban los duques dos dedos de parecer tontos, pues tanto ahinco ponían en burlarse de los tontos. (II, lxx, 1041)

> that he considers the mockers were as mad as their victims, and the Duke and Duchess within a hair's breadth of appearing fools themselves for taking such pains to play tricks on a pair of fools. (P. 916)

If the reader agrees with Cide Hamete's appraisal here, he is likely to reassess his judgment of the *eclesiástico*'s initial reproach to the Duke and Duchess. If he does so, however, it would seem that Cide Hamete's own adverse judgment of the chaplain must also be called into question. For the chaplain's condemnation of the Duke and Duchess's treatment of Don Quijote had seemed to be the main proof of his unsympathetic nature. Thus it appears that with regard to questions of value, not only is Cide Hamete reticent, but he is also liable to make unreliable choices.

Inclusionism

We have seen that, according to the criterion of relevance often voiced in the *Quijote*, that which does not serve "para sacar una verdad en limpio" is to be dismissed as digressive. But like judgments of value, judgments concerning what is relevant and what is digressive vary according to one's perspective. Recognizing this, Cardenio interrupts his tale with the following apology:

> No os canséis, señores, de oír estas digresiones que hago; que no es mi pena de aquellas que puedan ni deban contarse sucintamente y de paso, pues *cada circunstancia suya me parece a mí que es digna de un largo discurso*. (I, xxvii, 269; italics mine)

> Do not grow weary, gentlemen, of hearing these digressions of mine; for my grief cannot be told succinctly and methodically, since *every circumstance of it seems to me to deserve a long discourse*. (P. 232)

With regard to his own suffering, Cardenio considers no detail to be irrelevant; each is worthy of elaboration. Cide Hamete's subject is much larger than Cardenio's; it is reality itself. And from his perspective no narrative or detail is less valuable or less relevant than another. Hence, while Cardenio apologizes for what he has included, Cide Hamete laments about what he has been forced to exclude. He has reluctantly—and, as we have seen, only superficially—yielded to the criticisms of those readers of the first part who objected to what they considered to be digressive. But Cide Hamete, claiming to know better, begs the discerning reader not to blame him for what he has left out:

> se contiene y cierra en los estrechos límites de la narración, teniendo habilidad, suficiencia y entendimiento para tratar del universo todo, pide no se desprecie su trabajo y se le den alabanzas, no por lo que escribe, sino por lo que ha dejado de escribir. (II, xliv, 849)

> So, being confined and enclosed within the narrow limits of the story, though he has the skill, the knowledge and the capacity for dealing with the whole universe, he begs that his pains shall not be under-valued, and that he shall be praised not for what he writes, but for what he has refrained from writing. (P. 746)

I have said that Cide Hamete's subject is reality itself, and indeed he claims the capacity "para tratar del universo todo," "for dealing with the whole universe." His aim is encyclopedic. He does not distinguish between the essential and the digressive because *everything* is an essential part of the whole universe.

Cide Hamete's attempt to comprehend the universe involves not only the inclusion of details and narratives, but also the inclusion of various styles and literary kinds. It has been suggested that the *Quijote* is a veritable encyclopedia of "formas de la imaginación," that is, of various modes for the imaginative representation of reality.[7] And it would seem to be the function of Cide Hamete to offer these various "formas," such as those embodied in pastoral romance, Byzantine tales, and semi-realistic comedy, as part of his ambitious project. Just as he presents opposing moral perspectives, the heart of a story and the most trivial details, abiding characters and ephemeral ones, he shows us the world through various imaginative configurations, various literary fixes on reality.

The *Quijote* has often been seen as the first modern novel, partly, at least, on the basis of its passion for verisimilitude, particularly for the quotidian. Sancho, for example, unlike squires in chivalric literature, is concerned with his wages and his low comforts. From the point of view of chivalric literature, such concerns are mean as well as irrelevant to the truths of the chivalric world view. From the point of view of the inclusionist Cide Hamete, details, even low ones, are essential constituents of reality. So to the extent that the *Quijote* is a pioneering work of novelistic realism, it is one by dint of Cide Hamete's digressiveness, his refusal to exclude anything as unessential.[8] The realistic novel then is the invention of Cide Hamete. But just as Cide Hamete's inclusiveness produces the novel, his generic inclusiveness, paradoxically, moves him to present literary kinds that, unlike the realistic novel, include the fantastic and exclude the quotidian.

Cide Hamete's inclusiveness, as we have seen, strives to build the data of experience and the various imaginative configurations of those data into a unified picture of reality. But there is a distinct ironic distance between Hamete and Cervantes himself, and hence between Hamete's rambling narrative and the *Quijote* of Cervantes. Martínez-Bonati has argued convincingly that the "formas de la imaginación" are ironically juxtaposed in order to illuminate

> la verdad que no hay un absoluto de la imaginación humana; que para henchirse de vida, tiene que someterse a las limitaciones de una abstracción configuradora, de un "estilo."[9]

> the truth that there is no absolute of the human imagination, that in order to take life in, one has to submit oneself to the limitations of an abstract configuration, of a "style."

This ironic attitude, I submit, is directed at Cide Hamete's project as embodied in his book. Just as the presentation of opposing modes of apprehending reality undermines the adequacy of any mode, the presentation of opposing moral perspectives undermines the adequacy of any single judgment of value. Nor does any composite of moral or of modal perspectives achieve an adequacy that the individual perspectives lack. The ironic juxtaposition of Cervantes' *Quijote*, unlike the inclusionist project of Cide Hamete, does not transcend the limitations of each perspective by fusing them all into a totality.[10] The disturbing fact that the cave of the Caba Rumía is a good place to one person and an evil place to another does not yield any transcendent reconciliation of opposites. By the same token, the romantic idealism of one literary mode and the comic realism of another do not embrace one another. This stubborn resistance of perspectives to a reliable judgment of value, and of literary modes to any definitive choice of the proper imaginative configuration for the apprehension of reality is the key to the open form of the *Quijote*.

I said at the beginning of this chapter that the structure of the *Quijote* is not merely homologous with the doctrines enunciated in the novel, but that it is dictated by them. And the force of this claim can now be appreciated. A form that is orderly rather than digressive is founded, according to the *Quijote,* upon the principle of relevance to the truth. Details and events are subordinated to the guiding perspective, that of truth, and anything that cannot be subordinated to the expression of the truth can, in the service of truth, be excluded. But Cide Hamete does not know the truth. He can present conflicting perspectives, but cannot determine whether one is true and another false. Unable to impose a transcendent perspective, he is unable to control his material by subordinating the parts to such a perspective. His only hope is to include everything. But a narrative can never include everything. When guided by formalism, as in the case of James, it can exclude that which detracts from the *appearance* of unity. When guided by the principle of truth, but hampered by the inability to know the truth, it can only digress. Digressiveness, then, is not merely the emblem of the *Quijote's* epistemological dilemma, but the necessary embodiment of it. The form represents the state of affairs that engendered it.

Although Cide Hamete is concerned with grasping reality, Cervantes' subject is not reality itself, but the human efforts to comprehend it. Cide Hamete is a paradigm of human judgment and imagination and the *Quijote* is an ironic consideration of his efforts. It shows the inadequacies of the forms of imagination, of judgments of value, and of attempts to construct a whole out of a mass of details. While to Cide Hamete, the form of his narrative is open simply because he does not complete his impossibly grand project, because he fails to treat the universe in its entirety, the form of Cervantes' book is open because judgments and genres, tales and details break loose from one another and clash resoundingly. The form of the *Quijote bespeaks,* in the richest sense of that word, profound skepticism about the adequacy of each style, each assessment of value, each judgment of relevance. The form reflects and embodies Cide Hamete's grandiose failures.

Notes

1. Henry James, *The Art of the Novel* (New York: Scribners, 1934), p. 5.
2. Ibid.
3. II, xviii, 662. All page references to the *Quijote* are to the edition of Martín de Riquer

(Barcelona: Editorial Juventud, 1958). For the convenience of readers using other editions, part and chapter are also identified, in upper- and lower-case Roman numerals respectively. Subsequent references to the *Quijote* will be given in the text.

4. The English translations are those of J. M. Cohen (*The Adventures of Don Quixote* [London: Penguin, 1950]), with occasional modifications of my own at points where a more literal rendering is needed for the purposes of my argument. The page references for the Cohen translation are given in the text.

5. Cf. Rosalie Colie, *Paradoxia Epidemica* (Princeton: Princeton University Press, 1966).

6. The case of the cueva de Montesinos is a conspicuous exception to this rule. Here the Cide Hamete refuses to commit himself as to whether Don Quijote's account of the happenings in the cave is true, and leaves the judgment to the reader: "Tú letor, pues eres prudente, juzga lo que te pareciere, que yo no debo ni puedo más . . ." (II, xxiv, 713).

7. Félix Martínez-Bonati, "Cervantes y las regiones de la imaginación" in *Dispositio* 2 (Winter 1977): 42–43.

8. From the point of view of neoclassical criticism, of course, the romance itself was open to the charge of digressiveness. For although it was not inclusive in the studied and comprehensive manner of the *Quijote*, it did include multiple plots—something that, as in the dispute over Ariosto's *Orlando Furioso*, often aroused the ire of traditionalist critics. (See Bernard Weinberg, *A History of Literary Criticism in the Italian Renaissance*, 2 vols. [Chicago: University of Chicago Press, 1961], 2:954–1073.) And the controversy over Ariosto and the "romance," as Claudio Guillén points out, was "doubtless a background condition for the invention of *Don Quixote*" (*Literature as System: Essays Toward the Theory of Literary History* [Princeton: Princeton University Press, 1971], p. 109). The *Quijote* establishes itself as a countergenre then, not only by playing itself off against the romance, but also, to some extent, by building upon the romance's prior countergeneric relationship to the ideal epic.

9. Martínez-Bonati, "Cervantes y las regiones de la imaginación," p. 52.

10. For the term *inclusionism* and a survey of Renaissance writers and critics who saw a gathering of literary kinds as a way of overcoming the limitations of each kind, see Rosalie Colie, *The Resources of Kind: Genre-Theory in the Renaissance,* ed. Barbara K. Lewalski (Berkeley: University of California Press, 1973), pp. 76–102.

4

Thomson's *Seasons:*
Fragments and Order

Jedes Ding muß sich isolieren und isoliert werden, um etwas
zu sein. Indem der Verstand jeden Inhalt der Welt in eine feste
Bestimmtheit bannt und das flüssige Wesen gleichsam ver-
steinert, bringt er die Mannigfaltigkeit der Welt hervor, denn
die Welt wäre nicht vielseitig ohne die vielen Einseitigkeiten.
—Karl Marx, *Debatten über das Holzdiebstahlsgesetz*

Preliminary

Bacon's *Novum Organum* has provided us with a paradigm for
what could be called the teleological open form. Bacon's aphorisms betoken the present, fragmentary state of our scientific
knowledge, while the connectives between the aphorisms point
toward the ultimate pyramid of unified knowledge that Bacon's
new method will reveal. A less secular version of such a teleological open form can be found in Pascal's *Pensées,* where, on the one
hand, the disorder of our present knowledge reflects not merely
the state of our present progress, but the unalterable weakness of
man's rational faculties in his fallen state; but where, on the other
hand, there is a transcendent order, "le véritable ordre . . . qui
marquera toujours mon objet par le désordre même."[1] The apparently chaotic fragmentation of the *Pensées* is thus transformed by
the transcendent *ordre de la charité,* which "consiste princi-
palement à la digression sur chaque point qui a rapport à la fin,
pour la montrer toujours."[2] Thus, both in Bacon and in Pascal
there is an immediate disorder that points to an ultimate order, in
one case the complete knowledge of the natural world to be provided by an inductive method, and in the other the knowledge of
the *ordre de la charité,* which is reached partly by reason's inter-

pretation of its own limitations. Fragments point toward their ultimate unification; openness points toward closure.

The Seasons, distinguished on the one hand by discontinuous
descriptions of the natural world, by didactic and narrative digressions, and by tonal and generic variety, and on the other by a
theodicy that reveals the unity underlying and justifying the apparent disunity, seems eminently assimilable to either the Baconian or
the Pascalian model of the teleological open form, and perhaps to a
combination of the two. And in fact the fullest and most cogent
analysis of the poem—that of Ralph Cohen[3]—provides us with the
precise formulations that would facilitate such an assimilation. For
Cohen, the fragmentary form of the poem is to be understood in
terms of our fragmentary empirical knowledge of the world. Our
perceptions are fragmentary and are not rationally connected with
one another:

> The poem . . . deliberately avoided rational connections. It was com-
> posed of diverse fragments. . . . The world being perceivable only in
> fragments . . . no view of the whole could exist without an act of
> belief.[4]

In addition to representing the fragmentary world that is available
to us in the absence of an act of faith, the poem, in Cohen's view,
also urges its readers to engage in such an act of faith. Even with
such an act of faith, however, the fragments are not immediately
transformed into a unified whole, for faith in God is, in effect—
and here I am reformulating—faith in the future. The connections
that we now lack will be available to us in a future world:

> The "unifying vision" is that God's love and wisdom, only fragmentar-
> ily perceptible in the beautiful and dangerous aspects of man and na-
> ture, will become fully perceptible in a future world.[5]

The "unifying vision" is thus a glimpse of a future vision.

It is clear, I think, even from so brief a description of some of
Cohen's conclusions, that his reading of *The Seasons* places it
squarely in the realm of the teleological open form. In the poem, as
in the *Novum Organum,* the limitations of our empirical knowledge are expressed by means of fragments. But the *telos* that is
envisioned is not the culmination of empirical knowledge, but
rather, as in Pascal, the religious transcendence of it.

If we accept Cohen's reading, consequently, we may use *The
Seasons* to validate the paradigms of teleological open form already

established in these pages and to provide an eighteenth-century example of their partial fusion. Unfortunately, however, Cohen's reading—despite its merits—fits my paradigms better than it fits Thomson's poem. The poem, in fact, rather than belonging to the categories that I have already described, seems to establish a substantially new category of open form. It accomplishes this—and, in the process, challenges the adequacy of Cohen's reading— principally by means of a radical complication and, to an extent, transvaluation, of the relationship between fragmentation and unification, part and whole.

The Art of Differentiation

Thus far in our historical investigation of the open form, the valuation placed by our several authors upon epistemological fragmentation has been straightforward and consistent. Positive value resides in coherent, unified knowledge—whether of the natural world or the spiritual one—and fragmentation of knowledge is valued negatively. Fragmentary knowledge, sometimes remediable, sometimes not, is always defective knowledge.

And the same sort of valuation applies to the objects of our knowledge. If the fragmentation of the world is real, a result, say, of the Fall, then the world is defective; and if the fragmentation is only apparent, a result of our deficient understandings, then the world is *apparently* defective.

In *The Seasons*, the world is presented as discontinuous rather than unified, but the discontinuous parts are not valued negatively. Not that Thomson ascribes value to fragments; he simply does not see discontinuity as fragmentary. Instead of presenting the natural world in terms of the dichotomy of fragments versus wholes, Thomson invokes the dichotomy of chaos versus order, where order is represented, in the first place, not by coherent wholes but by discrete parts. Hence a series of discrete entities, which, in another context, could be seen as fragmentary and therefore negative in value, when placed in the context of the chaos/order dichotomy, represents order and positive value. This point is fundamental and will require some elaboration.

Dr. Johnson defined Chaos as "the mass of matter, supposed to be in confusion before it was divided by the creation into its proper classes and elements."[6] This formulation is clearly based on the account of creation in *Genesis*, where we are presented not with the *ex nihilo* creation stipulated by later theology, but with the division of a primordial mass into parts: the division of light from dark, of waters from the firmament. What the biblical account and Dr. Johnson's dictionary entry provide us, of course, is not merely a definition of chaos, but also a notion of its contrary—order. If chaos is a confused mingling, then order involves differentiation, a separation into parts.

This Judeo-Christian dichotomy between chaos and order is, I believe, closely paralleled by the Greek notions of the unlimited and the limited. For the Pythagoreans, Limit *(peras)* and the Unlimited *(apeiron)* were "set at the beginning of things as the two contrasting principles by which the world evolved."[7] As with the other pairs of opposites that, for the Pythagoreans, made the world, one member of the pair was valued positively and the other negatively; in this case *peras* was the good and *apeiron* the evil.[8] This valuation is explained by G. N. Giordano Orsini in terms of the Greek preference for the well-defined, the clearly bounded and limited, and hence the shapely and well-formed:

> On one side we have the vast, indeterminate nondescript stuff out of which everything is made; but on the other side, we have the Limit, i.e., definiteness of shape and size, and eventually even of configuration and structure. Bring them together, and the whole ordered universe of things and beings comes into view, each thing marked out within its boundaries.[9]

This formulation, as Orsini goes on to point out, allows us to see why modern scholars have found in the Pythagorean dyad of Unlimited and Limit the root of the Aristotelian categories of Matter and Form.[10] Lancelot Law Whyte, for example, in his "Chronological Survey on Form," observes that with the Pythagoreans

> the conception of form as the characteristic principle of a thing begins to appear, correlative to the conception of matter. The limit gives form to the unlimited.[11]

I have said that the Unlimited (Matter)/Limited (Form) dichotomy resembles the Hebrew dichotomy of Chaos and Order. And the most obvious similarity between the two dichotomies lies in the nature of their positive poles. For whether called *Limit, Form, Order,* or *Differentiation,* the good in both dyads is that which is set off, that which is clearly distinguishable, that which manifests its individual identity. The negative poles, on the other hand, do not seem to resemble one another so strongly as the positive poles. But both their similarities and their differences bear on a correct understanding of *The Seasons* and therefore need to be considered here. Insofar as *Chaos* is taken to connote a confused mingling, as in Dr. Johnson's definition,[12] it would seem to allow at least some recognition of elements that need to be clearly distinguished from one another. The more abstract notion of the Unlimited, on the other hand, lacking even indistinct or confused recognition, seems to connote merely a blank boundlessness. But this blank boundlessness, like the chaos of mingling, may conceivably contain already existing but not yet discernible elements. The blankness could be a sort of intensified mingling in which the confused things are not even partially recognizable. The uniformity of the Unlimited would then be only apparent, and the difference between blank undifferentiation and the chaos of mingling would in reality be one of degree.

Now, the conception of order as differentiation, shared by both the Hebrew and Greek dyads, operates, as we shall see, in *The Seasons,* and in fact lies at the heart of the thematic and formal structure of the poem. The value placed on differentiation in the poem is established by means of a contrast with the disorder that occurs when distinctions are blurred or effaced. Thomson presents two versions of this disorder, namely, confused mingling, in which distinctions are blurred, and total undifferentiation, in which the various entities merge into an *apparently* uniform mass. Moreover, these two sorts of disorder are presented as part of a single continuum in which blank undifferentiation is seen as simply an extreme version of confused mingling, a version in which individual entities, first seen indistinctly, become totally indistinguishable. Thus Thomson uses the negative poles of both the Hebrew and the Greek dyads as part of a single process that serves to set off the differentiated order that both dyads share.

Before we look at the actual passages in the poem that establish this structure of order and disorder, we need to engage in some preliminary considerations that will help us, in a somewhat *a priori* manner, to determine how literally these passages ought to be read. The effacement of distinctions in *The Seasons* is effected by certain natural phenomena such as fog, night, and storms, phenomena that periodically obscure differences, but, in most cases, do so only temporarily. Because the forces that oppose differentiation in the poem are regular and familiar features of nature, one might be tempted to see them not as presenting genuine instances of disorder, but merely as evocations or metaphors of the primordial Chaos out of which the present order of differentiation emerged. For although these forces are sometimes destructive, for the most part they do not affect the ontological integrity of the distinct objects that constitute the order of differentiation. The various objects, that is, are still there; we just cannot see them.

But the fact that in *The Seasons* individual objects usually remain intact does not allow us to conclude that the disorder depicted in the poem is not at the same time real disorder. The reason that preservation of ontological integrity in Thomson's depictions of disorder cannot serve to set them apart from primordial disorder is simply that primordial disorder itself, as our analysis has shown, does not depend on a lack of ontological integrity. For both chaotic mingling and blank undifferentiation have as their defining characteristic mere indistinguishability. Indeed things may be indistinguishable from one another in a tactile sense, because they are intertwined or otherwise jumbled together, but they may also be indistinguishable visually, because they are "shrouded," for instance, by darkness. Moreover, accounts of Creation provide strong hints that Chaos is to be understood in terms of the indiscernibility occasioned by the lack of light. In the Hebrew account of creation—and indeed, according to Ernst Cassirer, in most creation myths—"the process of creation merges with the dawning of the light."[13] If order is a function of differentiation, then light is one of the first products of differentiation precisely because—as Thomson was acutely aware—it is an instrument of further differentiation: light, in illuminating things, distinguishes them from one another. Since light procures order, darkness, which obscures things without otherwise damaging them, is a source of disorder. And if disorder is a function of the imperceptibility of distinctions, as it is in Thomson's poem, then it is pointless to distinguish "real" disorder from "perceptual" disorder.

The fact that such phenomena as night and fog serve in *The Seasons* as actual instances of disorder would not be altogether surprising to students of myth. For in numerous myths there is a periodic recurrence of Chaos and of Creation. Mircea Eliade has shown that the beginning of the new year is seen, in various cultures, as a repetition of Creation—not simply a reminder or evocation, but an actual recurrence of it.[14] And such recurrences are preceded by recurrences of Chaos, which Eliade characterizes in precisely those perceptual terms which I have used here: "[T]here is a return to . . . the inauguration of a 'nocturnal' regime in which limits, contours, distances, are indiscernible."[15] But although the perceptual nature of Chaos in these recurrences tends to confirm the notion that Thomson's "nocturnal regimes" are no mere analogues of disorder, it in no way entails that these "regimes" are seen by Thomson as actual repetitions of the original Chaos. For to be able to consider a regime in which limits and contours are indiscernible to be an actual recurrence of primordial Chaos (or in order to see the dawn or the coming of spring as a real Creation[16]), one would need not only to understand Chaos in terms of imperceptibility—which Thomson does—but also to be able to suspend notions of concrete time in such a way as to allow the same event to occur more than once—and this Thomson does not do. Thomson does not have a mythic, ahistorical sense of time. The creation was *then,* not *now.* Thomson explicitly indicates that instances of natural, recurrent disorder are *like* the primordial Chaos, allowing us to infer that they are not identical with it.

We may conclude then that although the "nocturnal" regimes in Thomson, those situations in which the distinctions between things are obscured by natural forces, are genuine instances of disorder, they are not mythic recurrences of primordial Chaos. The instances of disorder in *The Seasons,* as we shall see, stand in a metaphorical relationship to the original Chaos, but it is a metaphor in which one instance of disorder stands for another, archetypal one. For these reasons I shall refer to the recurrent disorders of nature (whether they resemble the primordial Chaos of mingling or that of blank undifferentiation) as instances of *chaos* (lower case). Having said this much by way of prolegomenon, I may proceed to the textual evidence upon which many of the foregoing remarks have been based.

Mingling and mixing in *The Seasons* are particularly associated with the terror and confusion of storms. A sea storm, for example, is

> . . .a mingled mass
> Of roaring winds and flame and rushing floods.[17]

In a thunderstorm we find the roar

> Enlarging, deepening, mingling, peal on peal
> Crushed horrible, convulsing heaven and earth.
> (*Summer,* 1142–43)

Dark winter rains

> Drive through the mingling skies with vapour foul
>
> *(Winter,* 74)

If such mingling suggests the Hebrew Chaos of confusion, it moves imperceptibly into the total undifferentiation characteristic of the Unlimited:

> The weary clouds,
> Slow meeting, mingle into solid gloom.
>
> *(Winter,* 202–3)

Although the mingling of these storms seems to be merely that of the elements of the storms themselves, other manifestations of the terrible side of nature do not merely exemplify chaos in themselves, but also carry chaos to the landscape that they act upon. In the autumn flood, for example,

> Herds, flocks, and harvests, cottages and swains
> Roll mingled down.
>
> *(Autumn,* 340–42)

But as with the elements of the natural forces themselves, the chaos that is effected upon the landscape may be that of total undifferentiation, in which things simply lose their individual identities. And, in fact, it is this sort of chaos, the sort that blots out distinctions without leaving a trace, that appears most often in the poem. In several passages this chaos—as opposed to that of mere mingling—strongly establishes the status of differentiation as a principle of order.

A clear example is to be found in the description of the fog in *Autumn* (695–735). The fog first rolls around the hill (710), then covers the mountain, obscuring the variety afforded by its prospects. As

> The huge dusk gradual swallows up the plain,
>
> (718)

the woods vanish. The first general effect is to make objects appear indistinct and unnatural:

> Indistinct on earth,
> Seen through the turbid air, beyond the life
> Objects appear.
>
> (724–26)

But finally indistinctness gives way to a total undifferentiation:

> at last,
> Wreathed dun around, in deeper circles still
> Successive closing, sits the general fog
> Unbounded o'er the world, and mingling thick,
> A formless grey confusion covers all.
>
> (727–31)

Thus the biblical process has been reversed, and, metaphorically, Chaos has come again. And indeed, in the subsequent lines Thomson explicitly compares the formless gray confusion with the biblical Chaos:

> As when of old (so sung the Hebrew bard)
> Light, uncollected, through the Chaos urged
> Its infant way, nor order yet had drawn
> His lovely train from out the dubious gloom.
>
> (732–35)

Fog is thus like Chaos in that it blots out the distinctions between things, merging them in an undifferentiated mass. And since the total lack of distinctions, total undifferentiation, results from the gradual obscuring of distinctions, its formlessness, for Thomson, is simply an extreme version of the chaos of mingling. In the biblical Chaos, by the same token, light was an "infant," still "uncollected," that is, not distinguished from darkness and gathered together; and the individual entities that constitute order had not yet been drawn from the "dubious gloom," not yet, that is, made perceptible as discrete things. The similarity between the effacement of "great variety" by the fog, and the effacement of things in the biblical Chaos, a sort of mirror-image in which the temporal relationship is reversed, is so great that Thomson's simile might perhaps be faulted for being too obvious and hence unilluminating. But it is valuable insofar as it shows that Thomson was acutely conscious of the association of differentiation with order and of the effacement of difference with disorder.

A somewhat more paradoxical example of the same set of associations is provided in Thomson's description of the night. Insofar as the first ordering during the Creation was accomplished by the separation of light from darkness, and hence of day from night, night is a discrete thing, the product of differentiation. Night's status as one of the first products of ordering, in fact, presumably helps to explain why Milton saw fit to include it in his heaven.[18] Nonetheless, in addition to being a product of differentiation, night is also an effacer of distinctions, and hence is associated with chaos:

> Sunk in the quenching gloom,
> Magnificent and vast, are heaven and earth.
> Order confounded lies, all beauty void,
> Distinction lost, and gay variety
> One universal blot—such the fair power
> Of light to kindle and create the whole.
>
> (*Autumn*, 1139–44)

The similarity between night and fog is obvious. Insofar as night quenches distinctions, it, like fog, confounds order and voids beauty. The blending of discrete entities into a uniform whole, "one universal blot," is the opposite of order. Light, conversely, seems to be associated with order, but its status too is ultimately paradoxical. On the one hand, light is able to "kindle and create" the world of order, presumably merely insofar as it frees things from quenching darkness, merely insofar as it differentiates the various entities from one another. Yet, as we shall see below, light contains its own chaos.

Winter, like night, is a product of differentiation, namely, the division of the year into four seasons; but, at the same time, also like night, it is an effacer of differentiations. Its characteristic force, snow, blots out distinctions, and hence provides another version of chaos. Here, however, the blotting is not always associated with darkness and gloom, but may be effected by brightness and purity:

> The cherished fields
> Put on their winter-robe of purest white.
> 'Tis brightness all . . .
> . . . .
> Earth's universal face, deep-hid and chill,
> Is one wild dazzling waste, that buries wide
> The works of man.
>
> (*Winter*, 232–40)

But at other times snow is allied with darkness and, of course, may efface not only the works of man but also the natural world and man himself. Witness the description of the doomed swain lost in a snowstorm:

> All Winter drives along the darkened air,
> In his own loose-revolving fields the swain
> Disastered stands; sees other hills ascend,
> Of unknown joyless brow; and other scenes;
> Of horrid prospect, shag the trackless plain;
> Nor finds the river nor the forest, hid
> Beneath the formless wild; but wanders on
> From hill to dale.
>
> *(Winter,* 277–83)

In being hidden beneath the "formless wild," the discrete features of the landscape become part of this formless wild. Lacking form itself, the snowstorm "deforms"[19] the world; that is, it deprives the world of form.

Ralph Cohen has noted that "*Winter* has as its recurrent image the loss of form, shape, mould, order."[20] And if this loss of form is understood—as the evidence cited thus far suggests it should be— in terms of the blotting-out of distinctions, the conversion of variety into blank uniformity, then the significance of the opening line of *Winter,*

> See, Winter comes to rule the varied year,

becomes clearer. Winter rules the varied year precisely insofar as it has the power to efface its variety.

If winter is characterized by deformation, by the obliteration of variety, then spring is the season in which distinctions reappear, in which variety reasserts itself. In *Winter,* even mountains had been effaced, piled into chaos by the snows:

> Undissolving from the first of time,
> Snows swell on snows amazing to the sky;
> And icy mountains high on mountains piled
> Seem to the shivering sailor from afar,
> Shapeless and white, an atmosphere of clouds.
> Projected huge and horrid o'er the surge,
> Alps frown on Alps; or, rushing hideous down,
> As if old Chaos was again returned,
> Wide-rend the deep and shake the solid pole.
>
> *(Winter,* 904–12)

In the spring thaw, obliterating snows are removed, and the mountains are once again differentiated from their surroundings and from one another:

> While softer gales succeed, at whose kind touch,
> Dissolving snows in livid torrents lost,
> The mountains lift their green heads to the sky.
>
> (*Spring*, 15–17)

But even in spring, chaos may strike again, providing a counterpoint to the descriptions of the various discrete features of nature—as if to remind us of the value of differentiation:

> And winter oft at eve resumes the breeze,
> Chills the pale morn and bids his driving sleets
> Deform the day delightless.
>
> (*Spring*, 19–21)

To show that *The Seasons* associates merging and uniformity with disorder, and differentiation with order, I have thus far concentrated on Thomson's rendering of the obliteration of differences. But the value of differentiation is also established in other ways. An interesting example is to be found in Thomson's treatment of light. On the one hand, light, as opposed to the darkness that effaces distinctions, has, as I have already noted, the power to "kindle and create" the variety of distinct objects that constitutes the visible world (*Autumn*, 1144). Light is, in fact,

> Nature's resplendent robe,
> Without whose vesting beauty all were wrapt
> In unessential gloom.
>
> (*Summer*, 92–94)

It is thus an ordering principle, a source of differentiation. Without light, things would lack their essences, would not be what they are. But in itself, light, as Newton had shown, is a complex, made up of mingled colors. And in this respect, it is in the differentiated elements, rather than in the blended whole, that the positive value resides:

> Here, awful Newton, the dissolving clouds
> Form, fronting on the sun, thy showery prism;

> And to the sage-instructed eye unfold
> The various twine of light, by thee disclosed
> From the white mingling maze.
>
> (*Spring*, 208–12)

Newton's "disclosure" is thus an unraveling, an ordering, and the "mingling maze" of light, a sort of chaos of undifferentiation. This view of the significance of Newton's prismatic analysis of light had already been expressed, somewhat more explicitly, in Thomson's "To the Memory of Sir Isaac Newton" (1727):

> Nor could the darting beam of speed immense
> Escape his swift pursuit, and measuring eye.
> E'en light itself, which everything displays,
> Shone undiscovered, till his brighter mind
> Untwisted all the shining robe of day;
> And from the whitening undistinguished blaze,
> Collecting every ray into his kind
> To the charmed eye educed the gorgeous train
> Of parent colors.

Here, white light, where colors are mingled, is "undistinguished," and the analysis of it into its separate colors is characterized as an untwisting. The "robe of day," which, in *Summer*, becomes the "resplendent robe" that, as we have just seen, displays the variety of nature, here is seen to contain its own variety. And this variety consists of a "gorgeous train / Of parent colors," foreshadowing the "lovely train" of differentiated things that in *Autumn* (735) will be drawn from Chaos. In the same Chaos passage (*Autumn*, 732), light will be described as "uncollected" before its separation from darkness; here, in "Isaac Newton," the division of light into its constituent colors involves "Collecting every ray into its kind." Thus, the "prism" passage from "Isaac Newton," not only in its substance, but even in its diction, contains keys to the parallels, in *The Seasons*, between the division of light into the colors of the spectrum, the division of the visible world into distinct objects, and the divisions that drew Order from Chaos. In addition, the passage plays with the paradoxes that these parallels entail, and that, in *The Seasons*, are only implicit: light, whose division from darkness is the beginning of order, and which, in turn, divides nature into distinct objects, remained itself undivided until subjected to Newton's genius.[21]

Differentiation and Harmony

In demonstrating that the discontinuities of nature in *The Seasons* betoken order, and hence are valued positively, I have attempted to counter Ralph Cohen's view that these discontinuities point to fragmentation and hence defectiveness. But Cohen adduces evidence to support his reading, and unless I am willing to content myself with having shown that Thomson's celebrated eclecticism can yield contradictory interpretations, I need to account for those features of the poem which seem to suggest that the world is fragmented.

The chief support, as far as I can tell, for the view that nature is represented as fragmented and hence defective, comes from the poem's accounts of the relationships of the natural world to its idyllic past and to its idyllic future. In *Spring* we are presented with the classical myth of the Golden Age, a time when

> Great Spring . . .
> Greened all the year; and fruits and blossoms blushed
> In social sweetness on the self-same bough.
> Pure was the temperate air; an even calm
> Perpetual reigned, save what the zephyrs bland
> Breathed o'er the blue expanse.
>
> (320–25)

The Golden Age is thus a period of uniformity and harmony, in which there is no alternation of colors or of seasons. Green, the color that traditionally joins light and shade, reigns all year in an unchanging Spring.

The passing of the Golden Age, of course, yields a fallen, corrupt world, and the mark of its corruption is alternation:

> But now, of turbid elements the sport,
> From clear to cloudy tossed, from hot to cold,
> And dry to moist, with inward-eating change,
> Our drooping days are dwindled down to naught,
> Their period finished ere 'tis well begun.
>
> (*Spring*, 331–35)

Since the Golden Age knew only spring, the alternation of the seasons themselves is, of course, a consequence of the Fall—or the pagan version of it. Under this conception, the cycle of the four seasons cannot have its conventional import as a symbol of totality, but rather seems to lend itself to the view that fragmented nature is the counterpart to fallen man. And it is this reading that Cohen, in fact, derives from Thomson's account of the Golden Age:

> The excessive passion which, in man, was an indication of the fall is analogically related to the fragmentation of nature—"the deep-cleft disparting Orb." . . . The seasons themselves are instances of a broken world.[22]

The problem with the Golden Age passage is that, while it appears to support Cohen's thesis, it does not appear to be consistent with the rest of the poem. It has often been observed by critics that the role of the Golden Age myth in *The Seasons* is inconsistent with the poem's theme of progress.[23] More significant for our purposes, however, is the apparent inconsistency between the doctrine of the Fall and of natural degeneration—whether in Hebrew or pagan guise—and the theodicy found elsewhere in the poem. Although there may be a question as to the extent to which unaided man is capable of interpreting God's purposes, of reading the book of nature, there is little question, outside of the Golden Age passage, that nature, however inscrutable it may sometimes seem, is the expression of God's perfection:

> [God] ceaseless works alone, and yet alone
> Seems not to work; with such perfection framed
> Is this complex, stupendous scheme of things.
>
> (*Spring*, 856–58)

Nature proclaims its divine authorship and sings its Author's praises. Even if men were silent, God's

> works themselves would raise a general voice;
> Even in the depth of solitary woods,
> By human foot untrod.
>
> (*Summer*, 187–89)

The poet of *The Seasons* considers his task to be that of reading the book of nature and imitating it:

> To me be Nature's volume broad displayed;
> And to peruse its all-instructing page,

> Or haply catching inspiration thence,
> Some easy passage, raptured, to translate,
> My sole delight.
>
>   (*Summer*, 192–96)

Nor is there any indication that the perfection that external nature displays consists merely of traces of a prelapsarian world whose glory may be apprehended even in its ruins.

The notion that nature has degenerated is opposed not only by the language of the passages just quoted, but also by the concept, repeatedly invoked in the poem, of the chain of being.[24] According to the doctrine of the chain of being, as A. O. Lovejoy has demonstrated,[25] the structure of nature is logically necessary; it is not even dependent on God's will. According to this view, a break in the chain, a degeneration, a shift toward a greater amount of evil or disorder in the world, is a logical impossibility.[26] The sort of theodicy that explains defects of nature as a consequence of man's disobedience tends to be diametrically opposed to the sort that sees apparent evil as part of a universal scheme.

In view of the apparent inconsistency between the Golden Age passage and the rest of the poem, a case could be made for treating the passage as an anomaly, a misplaced literary adornment included merely because of its venerable history. In fact, it has often been observed that the doctrine of original sin is out of fashion in eighteenth-century thought, having become—owing partly, at least, to its incompatibility with the precepts of deism—somewhat quaint and anachronistic.[27] And the Golden Age passage of *The Seasons*, insofar as it is seen as an embarrassing anomaly, reflects the more general role of the Fall during that period. However, although one may be convinced that the order of differentiation is central to the poem and the Golden Age passage is not, it is not necessary to read the passage out of the poem. But before we can ascertain its proper role in the poem, we need to relate the Golden Age passage to other passages that seem to support Cohen's reading.

I have said that the chief support for Cohen's view that nature in *The Seasons* is fragmented seems to lie in the contrast between present nature and the unity of an idyllic past and an idyllic future. And having introduced the Golden Age of the past, I now need to examine the idyllic future. The state of future bliss that Thomson evokes, while often framed in the religious language of revelation and immortality, is not strictly one of translunar paradise. Rather it is a vision of what Alan Dugald McKillop has called "empirical immortality."[28] In the works of several early eighteenth-century writers, "the future life comes to be seen in rational rather than mystic terms."[29] John Ray, for example, opined that in the future life we "shall be busied and employed in contemplating the Works of God and observing the Divine Art and Wisdom manifested in the Structure and Composition of them."[30] This view of our future knowledge is essentially the one that Thomson takes, particularly at the end of *Winter* and in the *Hymn.* When man is reborn, "from pain and death/ Forever free," he will come to understand things which, in his mortal state, were beyond his ken:

> The great eternal scheme,
> Involving all, and in a perfect whole
> Uniting as the prospect spreads,
> To reason's eye refined clears up apace.
>
> (*Winter,* 1046–49)

Naturally, the details of this future knowledge can scarcely be described, but Thomson can at least assure us that all the parts of the world will, in our new understanding, be united "in a perfect whole." The mark of this perfect whole is harmony, which is achieved by an orderly mingling of parts. Such harmony is at the center of the *Hymn,* which is permeated by the language of blending—elements are "mixed," "combined," "joined," "mingled," or "united." The following passage is representative:

> Mysterious round! what skill, what force divine,
> Deep-felt in these appear! a simple train,
> Yet so delightful mixed, with such kind art,
> Such beauty and beneficence combined,
> Shade unperceived so softening into shade,
> And all so forming an harmonious whole
> That, as they still succeed, they ravish still.
>
> (21–27)

(Despite the duplication of vocabulary, however, this orderly, harmonious blending, as we shall see, is not to be confused with the stormy, chaotic blending with which the order of differentiation is contrasted.)

The world, then, when we come to have a more perfect knowledge of it, will be seen to be, like the world of the Golden Age, harmonious and unified. However, the fact that the Golden Age of the past and the cognitive heaven of the future are characterized by a harmonious unity does not require that we see the presently observable world as fragmentary. For the orderly differentiation that we have observed in Thomson's representation of nature is quite compatible with the harmonious order that surrounds it. The two are, in fact, part of a single process.

"The Greek genius in thought and art," according to W. K. C. Guthrie,

> represents the triumph of λόγος or *ratio*, which has been defined as meaning on one hand, the intelligible, determinate, measurable, as opposed to the fantastic, vague, and shapeless, and on the other "the proportions of things both in themselves and as related to a whole."[31]

These two aspects of *logos* clearly constitute the source of the two principles of order that inform Thomson's poem—the order of differentiation and the order of harmonious unity. The natural world is marked by differentiation, the division into the intelligible, determinate, and measurable—a differentiation that, however, is often blurred into chaos by the effacing power of darkness, snow, and storm. The ultimate knowledge that we shall obtain in our immortal state, on the other hand, will reveal the other order, the integrative one, in which the separate parts relate to one another and to the whole in such a way as to constitute a total harmony.

It is important to recognize that these two orders are neither mutually dependent nor mutually independent, but rather have a relationship of asymmetrical dependency. The order of harmonious unity has as its precondition the order of differentiation. For a unity whose constituent parts were not clearly distinguishable from one another would, according to our analysis, be the same as chaos. The harmonious order is distinguished from chaos not by its unity per se, but by its unity in variety, by the fact that its unity is achieved without effacing its constituent parts. This is the basis for the distinction in *The Seasons* between the two kinds of mingling: the chaotic mingling that effaces distinctions, and the harmonious mingling that will be the object of our transcendent knowledge. The order of differentiation, in contrast to that of unity, has no other order as its precondition. As long as things are distinct and limited, the order of differentiation has been achieved.

Now, since the order of harmonious unity includes the order of differentiation as merely one of its defining characteristics, the former is necessarily more complex than the latter. Whether this fact, that the order of harmonious unity is more *complex* than the order of differentiation, necessarily entails that it constitutes a *higher* principle is an interesting question with great import for aesthetics in general and for the aesthetics of discontinuous forms in particular,[32] but it is a question that cannot be dealt with here. However, it is safe to say at least that Thomson himself did consider the more complex principle to be the higher one. After all, the order of differentiation can be perceived by ordinary mortals, without the advantage of cognitive immortality, while the harmonious order cannot. The order of differentiation demonstrates God's power to dispel chaos. The contemplation of the order of harmonious unity, however, provides solutions to the deepest mysteries of the universe; it allows the knowing soul to grasp the divine purpose.

The disorders and orders of the universe, as represented in *The Seasons*, thus form themselves into a dialectical pattern. At the bottom is Chaos, characterized by the absence of distinction, by a unity that has no parts. Next comes the order of differentiation, the separation of the primal unity into discrete parts. (At this stage, the obliterating force of chaos reasserts itself regularly, helping us to recognize the order that it is opposing, but also, as will become clearer in the sequel, taking its place as part of that order.) The second stage is represented by the physical universe, the world that we sense, experience, and interpret, and that is the subject of the bulk of the descriptions and ruminations making up *The Seasons*. Finally, at the highest stage, there is a new unity in which the parts that had been rescued from the unity of Chaos, while remaining distinct from one another, are reintegrated into a harmonious whole.

The Golden Age, of course, complicates this dialectical progression by placing in the distant past an analogue of the cognitive *telos* toward which we are moving. But this procedure is not uncommon in such cosmological myths. To quote a more recent version,

> We shall not cease from exploration
> And the end of our exploring
> Will be to arrive where we started
> And know the place for the first time.[33]

Illumination, like other sorts of progress, is often a return, and the Golden Age, with its prefigurement of the eschatological paradise that awaits us, complicates things in a way befitting the poem. The Golden Age consisted of unbounded spring, but it was not unbounded in the way chaos is. Its unity had articulation, and its boundlessness had the determinacy of a circle. The paradoxical fact that the progress to a cognitive heaven outside of time is also a return to a harmonious primitive past, is matched by the paradox that this heaven needs, by dint of its endlessness, partially to resemble chaos in order to go beyond both chaos and its opposite. The conclusion of the four *Seasons* manages to encapsulate these paradoxes in a single, summary line, thus closing a circle by opening the way to its transcendence. The storms of wintry time will quickly pass,

And one unbounded Spring encircle all.

The structure of *The Seasons,* as Cohen had correctly observed, imitates the structure of our knowledge of the natural world. Both the poem and the world as we know it are discontinuous, consisting of a variety of parts that are radically distinct from one another. But just as the discontinuity of the world, as it turns out, constitutes an orderly differentiation of its parts, the discontinuity of the poem, with its arbitrary catalogues of natural objects, its didactic and narrative digressions, its tonal and generic variety, must be seen as representing not fragmentation but the order of differentiation.

It is easy to guess why Thomson chose a form that imitates the order of differentiation rather than the higher order of harmony. The order of harmony is, after all, a transcendent one. Reason (as we shall soon see in greater detail) tells us of its existence, but its nature—the specific links that join the distinct entities of creation into a divine scheme—are not accessible to us in our present state. Consequently, although we may advert to the order of harmony, we cannot describe it. Moreover, the order of harmony, unlike the unified knowledge that Bacon foresaw but could not specifically describe, differs from the present state of our knowledge not in degree, but in kind. It is not the completion of a process that has already begun, but it involves an entirely distinct process, in which integration supplants differentiation. The order of harmony, in fact, corresponds not only to the apex of Bacon's pyramid of natural knowledge but also to the moral order, which, for Bacon, was accessible only by means of revelation, and was absolutely excluded from the realm of the new organon. *The Seasons* describes the world that is accessible to us—even the anticipation of harmony is placed outside the four seasons proper, in the *Hymn*— and the poem's form, rather than trying to anticipate the integrative order that will be unveiled in another life, accords with the differentiated order that we already possess.

Differentiation, Reason, and the Sublime

In the philosophical tradition that Thomson inherited, there is a familiar distinction between the combinatory and the analytic faculties of the mind. In Hobbes, the distinction is between fancy and judgment. Those who observe the "similitudes" between things

> are said to have a *good wit;* by which, in this occasion is meant *good fancy.* But they that observe their differences and dissimilitudes; which is called distinguishing, and discerning and judging between thing and thing; in case, such discerning be not easy are said to have *good judgment.*[34]

The fact that the activity of wit is a combinatory one, and that of judgment a separatory one is enunciated more explicitly by Locke:

> For *wit* lying most in the assemblage of *ideas,* and putting those together with quickness and variety, wherein can be found any resemblance or congruity, thereby to make up pleasant pictures and agreeable visions in the fancy: *judgment,* on the contrary, lies quite on the other side, in separating carefully, one from another, ideas wherein can be found the least difference, thereby to avoid being misled by similitude, and by affinity to take one thing for another.[35]

Now, if we apply this view of intellectual method to the cosmology that we have been discussing, we might say that insofar as judgment distinguishes between ideas or objects, separating them from one another, it serves to reveal the order of differentiation. The situation, on the other hand, in which things are mistaken for one another approximates the jumbled unity that constitutes chaos, and the function of judgment consequently resembles the divine process that educed Order from Chaos.[36]

In *The Seasons* the Judgment/Wit or Judgment/Fancy dichotomy is replaced by that of Reason (or Philosophy) and Fancy, but the essential distinction between the analytic function (Reason) and the synthetic (Fancy) remains intact. Reason and Philosophy are associated with distinctions and hence with the variety of things that constitute the order of differentiation:

> Sit beneath the shade . . .
> And pensive listen to the various voice
> Of rural peace—the herds, the flocks, the birds,
> The hollow-whispering breeze, the plaint of rills,
> That, purling down amid the twisted roots
> Which creep around, their dewy murmurs shake
> On the soothed ear. From these abstracted oft
> You wander through the philosophic world;
> Where in bright train continual wonders rise.
>
> (*Spring*, 914, 917–24)

Here the movement is from the perception (in this case auditory) of the variety and differentiation of the natural world to the invocation of a comparable variety in the philosophical world.

However, philosophy does not limit itself strictly to the discerning function of the judgment as described by Hobbes and Locke. It does not merely separate things from one another and discern the complexity of the world, but is able to move from this complexity to an apprehension of its source. It is

> intent to gaze
> Creation through; and, from that full complex
> Of never-ending wonders, to conceive
> Of the Sole Being right, who spoke the word,
> And Nature moved complete.[37]
>
> (*Summer*, 1784–88)

But this movement from the variety of the differentiated world to the unity of God is a movement through the differentiation, a movement by degrees. The philosophical variety of things is one in which the distinct objects differ from one another by degrees, and form a hierarchical chain. Reason moves along this chain and finds that it leads to God. Thomson conflates this movement up the chain of being with another traditional stage-by-stage progression, namely, the progression up the chain of causes:

> [Reason] up-tracing, from the dreary void,
> The chain of causes and effects to Him,

> The world-producing Essence, who alone
> Possesses being.
>> (*Summer*, 1745–48)

The chain of being culminating in God qua absolute Being and the chain of causes culminating in God qua first cause thus collapse into a single chain. Like the chain of causes, Bacon's methodical movement up a pyramid of more and more general axioms is also assimilated by Thomson to the movement up the chain of being. Bacon is seen as one who "led forth the true philosophy" (*Summer*, 1545)

> that slow ascending still,
> Investigating sure the chain of things,
> With radiant finger points to Heaven again.
>> (*Summer*, 1548–50)

The explanation for this series of conflations lies in the fact that philosophy in Thomson's scheme has a limited function, a function which, however, it sometimes threatens to overstep. Reason differentiates, and it builds upon this differentiation by moving, by degrees, from the various discrete things to a knowledge of their source, namely, God. But it cannot go beyond this function, it cannot explain the relationships among the various discrete objects constituting the world, for this would involve explaining God's purposes, thus entering the realm of final causes. The explanation of final causes, the explanation that makes apparent evil consistent with God's goodness and wisdom, however, is reserved for another stage of existence; it will be revealed to us in a future time, when

> what your bounded view, which only saw
> A little part, deemed evil is no more.
>> (*Winter*, 1066–67)

The chain of being, however, traditionally serves precisely this theodicean function by telling why an omnipotent and perfectly benevolent being made the world the way it is.[38] Consequently, there is a danger that this doctrine will short-circuit Thomson's dialectical scheme by allowing reason to reveal the order of harmony, an order which, according to this scheme, is supposed to be grasped only through eschatological revelation.[39] Thomson avoids this danger, however, by portraying the chain in terms of the order of differentiation, but not the order of harmony—that is, he reduces the chain to its form, that of a differentiated progress, which merges with the same form in chains of causes and in Bacon's method. He reduces it from an explanation of God's purpose to a vague index of God's role as creative source.

The order that is available to us mortals, the order of differentiation, is apprehended partly by means of the separatory function of reason, which, in turn, moves by degrees from a knowledge of the variety of the differentiated order to a knowledge of its source. But reason cannot then move back from that source to explain the true harmony that relates the differentiated parts of the world to one another. Reason is thus both an instrument for revealing the order of differentiation and a mediator between it and the order of harmony. By moving across the differentiated order that it reveals, reason allows us with "earnest eye" to

> anticipate those scenes
> Of happiness and wonder, where the mind,
> In endless growth and infinite ascent,
> Rises from state to state, and world to world.
>
> (*Winter*, 605–8)

Reason thus carries us to the threshold of the realm where the mind begins to acquire its knowledge of the order of harmony, but it does not allow us to pass that threshold.

The connection between the order of differentiation and the movement by degrees manifests itself not only in the movement from one individual entity or species[40] to the next, but even in the gradations to be found in single things or in general prospects. It even colors Thomson's representation of the natural sublime, that is, of those terrifying or awe-inspiring features of the natural world that the eighteenth century saw as evoking the power and boundlessness of the creator.

Consider, for example, the following passage, describing a prospect:

> Where the broken landscape, by degrees
> Ascending, roughens into rigid hills
> O'er which the Cambrian mountains, like far clouds
> That skirt the blue horizon, dusky rise.
>
> (*Spring*, 959–62)

The passage contains two characteristic features of the sublime— the brokenness, which in the conventions of the sublime, inspires terror; and the movement toward the horizon, which evokes infinity.[41] However, what, to my knowledge, is not conventional is the juxtaposition of the broken landscape with the movement by degrees. If brokenness and vastness are characteristic of the sublime insofar as they evoke awe, differentiation is not, precisely because, as Burke noted in 1757, differentiation implies clarity and order, and hence lacks the effect of the sublime (or "greatness," as it is called here):

> The mind is hurried out of itself, by a crowd of great and confused images; which affect because they are crowded and confused. For separate them, and you lose much of the greatness, and join them and you infallibly lose the clearness.[42]

The sublime thus resembles chaos; it thrives on disordered mingling instead of on separation. And if we recall the various passages from *The Seasons* that describe the deforming power of natural forces, we realize that they often serve not merely as contrasts to the order of differentiation, but as instances of the sublime. In quenching heaven and earth, for example, the night is "magnificent and vast." Chaotic forces, by dint of their power and boundlessness, bespeak God. Consequently, Milton can be praised in terms of the chaos that he described as well as in terms of his heaven:

> A genius universal as his theme,
> Astonishing as chaos, as the bloom
> Of blowing Eden fair, as heaven sublime.
> (*Summer,* 1569–71)

In the chaotic forces that periodically efface order, God shows his power by blotting out the very differentiations that He has created. But since these differentiations constitute the norm in nature, sublime scenes that are permanent features of the landscape are likely to have their awesomeness tempered with the differentiations that link them to the general order of things. And this, as we have just seen in the invocation of degrees in the prospect scene quoted above, is precisely what happens.

Nor is that passage unique in fulfilling this requirement. The waterfall passage of *Summer,* for example, which in the 1744 edition takes on new trappings of the sublime, also takes on, at the same time, new indications of differentiation:

I check my steps and view the broken scene.
   Smooth to the shelving brink a copious flood
Rolls fair and placid; where, collected all
In one impetuous torrent, down the steep
It thundering shoots, and shakes the country round.
At first, an azure sheet, it rushes broad;
Then, whitening by degrees as prone it falls,
And from the loud-resounding rocks below
Dashed in a cloud of foam, it sends aloft
A hoary mist and forms a ceaseless shower.
Nor can the tortured wave here find repose;
But raging still amid the shaggy rocks,
Now flashes o'er the scattered fragments, now
Aslant the hollow channel rapid darts;
And, falling fast from gradual slope to slope,
With wild infracted course and lessened roar
It gains a safe bed, and steals at last
Along the mazes of the quiet vale.

(Summer, 589–606)[43]

Here, once again, the language of brokenness and the evocation of terror are juxtaposed with the language of differentiation. The terrible falling water must whiten "by degrees," and then fall from "gradual slope to slope." These divisions by degrees not only make the terrible perhaps somewhat less terrible, but also suggest that just as reason moves upward to God by differentiated steps, the sublime in nature—when it is permanent rather than recurrent—evokes the greatness of God partly by reflecting the differentiation that He in the beginning imposed upon Chaos.

This sense that the sublime is linked to the order of differentiation is accented by the last lines of the passage, in which the same river whose fall has provided a scene of sublime horror "steals at last" into the "quiet vale." Just as the sublime is linked with the differentiated order of general nature by its internal divisions, its gradations, it is also linked physically to general order and gradually gives way to it.

Brokenness, moreover—the scattered fragments and the infracted course—here enters the service of order. The fragment, even when identified as such, is transmuted; it becomes a kind of differentiation, allied with gradation and opposing confusion. The broken part, by dint of its very distinctness, enters into a paradoxical synechdoche, and proclaims the glory of the whole.

Conclusion

The notion of chaos operative in *The Seasons,* as we saw in the second section of this chapter, is an extremely broad one: chaos obtains whenever natural forces render the distinctions between things imperceptible. Thus chaos includes such regular and conspicuous phenomena as night and winter. But night and winter, as we saw in the same section, are phenomena that, in addition to obscuring differences, are themselves products of differentiation, and hence part of a larger order. We saw, conversely, that light, which. functions to reveal differentiations, was, unless passed through Newton's prism, in itself undifferentiated and hence chaotic. In the fourth section we saw that the sublime in nature, which essentially fulfills the definition of chaos, nonetheless is differentiated and part of a larger order.

When we consider the paradoxical nature of all these examples of chaos we come to see that the very immanence of disorder in Thomson's scheme of things allows it to serve a theodicean purpose. For at the stage of the order of differentiation, every manifestation of chaos is differentiated from that which it opposes or that with which it alternates. Thus chaos serves not only to accentuate the very variety that it opposes, but also, by opposing variety, to become part of a more extensive variety. Chaos, rather than being identified as a mere disruption that needs to be minimized, finally is seen to enter into the order of differentiation and to be embraced as part of that order.[44]

Notes

1. Blaise Pascal, *Pensées,* in *Œuvres complètes,* ed. Louis Lafuma (Paris: Editions du Seuil, 1963), #532 (373). The number in parentheses in this reference and the subsequent reference indicates the number of the same fragment in the Brunschvicg edition.

2. *Pensées,* #298 (283).

3. Ralph Cohen, *The Unfolding of* The Seasons (Baltimore: Johns Hopkins University Press, 1970).

4. Ibid., pp. 326–27.

5. Ibid., p. 3.

6. *A Dictionary of the English Language,* 6th ed. (London, 1785).

7. W. K. C. Guthrie, *A History of Greek Philosophy,* 2 vols. (Cambridge: Cambridge University Press, 1962), 1:207.

8. Ibid.

9. G. N. Giordano Orsini, *Organic Unity in Ancient and Later Poetics: The Philosoph-*

ical Foundations of Literary Criticism (Carbondale: Southern Illinois University Press, 1975), pp. 12–13.

10. Ibid., p. 13.

11. Lancelot Law Whyte, ed., *Aspects of Form: A Symposium on Form in Nature and Art* (London: Lund Humphries, 1951), p. 230.

12. In Dr. Johnson's *Dictionary*, the second definition given for *Mingle* is "To contaminate; to make of dissimilar parts," and the exemplary quotation for this definition is from Milton:

> To confound the race
> Of mankind in one root, and Earth with Hell
> To mingle and involve.

Even *Blend*, which is today more clearly mejorative than *Mingle*, has as its second definition "To confound," with the following quotation from Hooker: "The moon should wander from her beaten way, the times and seasons of the year blend themselves by disordered and confused mixture."

13. Ernst Cassirer, *The Philosophy of Symbolic Forms*, trans. Ralph Mannheim, 3 vols. (New Haven: Yale University Press, 1955), 2: 96.

14. Mircea Eliade, *The Myth of the Eternal Return or, Cosmos and History*, trans. Willard R. Trask (Princeton: Princeton University Press, 1954), pp. 62–73.

15. Ibid., p. 69.

16. Cf. Cassirer's commentary on Herder's interpretation of the biblical Chaos: "For [Herder] the narrative of the creation is nothing other than the story of the birth of the light—as experienced by the mythical spirit in the rising of every new day, the coming of every new dawn. This dawning is for mythical vision no mere process; it is a true and original creation—not a periodically recurring natural process following a determinate rule, but something absolutely individual and unique. Heraclitus's saying, 'The sun is new each day,' is spoken in a truly mythical spirit." (*Philosophy of Symbolic Forms*, 2:97.)

17. Unless otherwise noted, citations from *The Seasons* are from the 1746 edition, the last published in the poet's lifetime. For this edition my text is that edited by James Sambrook in *The Seasons and The Castle of Indolence* (Oxford: Clarendon Press, 1972). For variants from earlier editions, I am using Sambrook's critical edition (Oxford: Clarendon, 1981).

18. See *Paradise Lost*, 5:628.

19. For an example of Thomson's own use of *deform* in this sense, see *Spring*, 20, quoted on p. 80 below.

20. Ralph Cohen, *Unfolding*, p. 253.

21. Cf. Marjorie Hope Nicolson, *Newton Demands the Muse: Newton's Optics and the Eighteenth-Century Poets* (Princeton: Princeton University Press, 1946), p. 28. Nicolson sees Thomson's mineral section (*Summer*, 140–59) as betokening the "resolution of light into colors, and the return of colors back to light."

22. Ralph Cohen, *Unfolding*, pp. 33–34.

23. See Alan Dugald McKillop, *The Background of Thomson's* Seasons (1942; reprint, Hamden, Conn.: Archon, 1961), p. 89.

24. See *Summer*, 334; *Spring*, 378; *Summer*, 1796–1805.

25. A. O. Lovejoy, *The Great Chain of Being: A Study of the History of an Idea* (Cambridge: Harvard University Press, 1936), passim.

26. Pope, in *An Essay on Man*, falls into this logical trap by scolding man for not being satisfied with his lot, with his place on the chain of being:

In Pride, in reas'ning Pride, our error lies;
All quit their sphere, and rush into the skies.
Pride still is aiming at the blest abodes,
Man would be Angels, Angels would be Gods.
Aspiring to be Gods, if Angels fell,
Aspiring to be Angels, Men rebel;
And who but wishes to invert the laws
Of ORDER, sins against th' Eternal Cause.

(1:123–30)

But Pope remains faithful to the doctrine of the chain to the extent that he omits any degeneration of external nature as an accompaniment to man's moral transgressions.

27. See, for example, Basil Willey, *The Eighteenth-Century Background: Studies on the Idea of Nature in the Thought of the Period* (1940; reprint, Boston: Beacon Press, 1961), pp. 46–48. Cf., however, Donald Greene, *The Age of Exuberance: Backgrounds to Eighteenth-Century English Literature* (New York: Random House, 1970), pp. 92–100. Greene claims that eighteenth-century English religio-ethical attitudes were predominantly Augustinian in character. This claim is based partly on evidence from earlier centuries, partly on doctrinal statements in Anglican documents that were still in widespread use during the period, and partly on an interesting premise concerning the force of religious education and the psychology of apostasy: "It is hard to see how, except by an act of conscious rejection (such as we have no reason to suppose that Swift or Johnson or most of their contemporaries among English writers ever made), anyone exposed to such doctrine week after week from earliest childhood, as the vast majority of the population of England were throughout the eighteenth century, could with conviction maintain either the Stoic view that human nature in itself provides a datum for morality, or the Pelagian one that man has some inherent good in himself and can, simply by industrious effort, lift himself by his moral bootstraps" (p. 97). Although the issue of which ideas were dominant in a given century can scarcely be settled in the space of a note, I think it would be appropriate at least to express some puzzlement at Greene's argument. Greene seems to be assuming that one must either consciously reject doctrines with which one has been raised or accept them lock, stock, and barrel. He seems to ignore the possibility that, while consciously considering oneself to be orthodox, one may assimilate and reflect current ideas that militate against orthodoxy—that one may modify one's beliefs without recognizing that one is doing so, or that one may hold contradictory views simultaneously. Moreover, in seeing the eighteenth century's purported Augustinianism as a continuation of the Augustinian trend in the Anglicanism of the two previous centuries, Greene seems to ignore the fact that even seventeenth-century Anglicanism was much more moderate and less Augustinian than the Calvinism against which it struggled, and that it was more moderate in practice than its own official positions would indicate. As a student of seventeenth-century English autobiography has observed, the Anglicans "preferred, while remaining committed officially to the Protestant view of justification by faith alone through grace, to grant man greater natural insight into spiritual truths and a larger share in his reconciliation to God" (Dean Ebner, *Autobiography in Seventeenth-Century England: Theology and the Self* [The Hague: Mouton, 1971], p. 74).

28. McKillop, *Background of Thomson's* Seasons, p. 22.

29. Ibid., p. 23. Cf. Ernest Lee Tuveson, *Millennium and Utopia: A Study in the Background of the Idea of Progress* (1949; reprint, New York: Harper Torchbooks, 1964), chap. 4.

30. *The Wisdom of God Manifested in the Works of the Creation*, quoted in McKillop, *Background of Thomson's* Seasons, p. 23.

31. Guthrie, *History of Greek Philosophy*, 1:205.

32. It is a question for aesthetics insofar as it bears on the status of complexity as an aesthetic norm. Notions of what constitutes order in the universe often provide the bases for notions of order in the arts. The order of harmonious unity, when applied to literature and called organic unity, has long reigned as the supreme aesthetic norm. Although the open form is not necessarily identified in terms of any actual degree of disunity, the fact that it needs to convey at least an impression of disconnectedness increases the likelihood that the aesthetic effect of the form will not come from any sense of harmonious unity. For this reason discontinuous works are likely to be judged aesthetically inferior or to be the focal point of diligent critical attempts to find hidden sources of unity or compensatory value. (Frank's efforts, discussed in chapter 1, to "spatialize" discontinuity may be seen to have been performed in the service of the norm of unity. For another example, see Erich Kahler, "The Disintegration of Artistic Form," in his *Out of the Labyrinth: Essays in Clarification* [New York: George Braziller, 1967]). The order of differentiation, however, when translated into an aesthetic norm—and the traditional norm of variety is the one that in *The Seasons* is associated with beauty and order—offers the basis for a positive valuation of the open form. Nonetheless, even when the form of open works is identified in terms of one kind of order as opposed to another, the precise aesthetic value of open works will still depend on whether the order of differentiation, being a less complex constituent of the order of harmonious unity, is an inferior sort of order. Hence the pertinence of an inquiry into the intrinsic value of complexity.

33. T. S. Eliot, *Little Gidding*, in *The Complete Poems and Plays: 1909–1950* (New York: Harcourt Brace, n.d.).

34. *Leviathan*, in *The English Works of Thomas Hobbes of Malmesbury*, ed. Sir William Molesworth (London: Bohn, 1869), 3:57.

35. John Locke, *An Essay Concerning Human Understanding*, bk. 2, chap. 11, section 2.

36. Cf. Nicolson, *Newton Demands the Muse*, p. 98: "The antithesis between Reason and Fancy could readily be expressed in terms of modern optics, since Fancy responded to 'imperfect,' 'faint,' 'confused,' sight, while Reason always saw clearly."

37. Ralph Cohen, playing down Thomson's praise of philosophy, claims that the poet stresses the limitations of reason. The world is fragmented because man's reason is incapable of making it whole. Hence the need for faith: "The conclusion is that philosophy cannot penetrate 'this dark state,' that only in the immortal state can the rising mind 'prove' God's love and wisdom, until then to be taken on faith" (*Unfolding*, pp. 171–72). The immediate basis for this conclusion is apparently to be found in the closing lines of *Summer*, which Cohen quotes just afterward:

> But here the Cloud,
> So wills ETERNAL PROVIDENCE, sits deep.
> Enough for us to know that this dark State,
> In wayward Passions lost, and vain Pursuits,
> This Infancy of Being, cannot prove
> The final Issue of the Works of God,
> By boundless LOVE and perfect WISDOM formed,
> And ever rising with the rising Mind.

However, in concluding that "only in the immortal state can the rising mind 'prove' God's love and wisdom," Cohen seems to be assuming that the "prove" in line 1802 is to be understood in the sense of "demonstrate to be a fact," and consequently that the poet is saying that mortals are incapable of establishing God's love and wisdom. But this reading is implausible. The subject of "prove" is this dark "State," which is also described as "this infancy of Being." Although it is conceivable that man's mortal state, his infancy of being, would, by dint of a metaphorical substitution, be characterized as being incapable of knowing something, it strikes me as more odd than poetic. It simply does not sound well to say that our present state cannot ascertain that something is the case. Moreover, even if we should assume that "Infancy of Being" stands for "Man, in his infancy of being," the logic of the consolation in the passage would be that it is sufficient for us to know that we cannot know. Such a sentiment would satisfy a Pyrrhonist, but would be quite unlikely to provide much consolation either to Thomson or to his contemporaries. These considerations, in themselves, do not prove that Cohen's reading of the passage is mistaken. However, the availability of an alternative reading that is free of these difficulties and consistent with Thomson's overall position renders Cohen's reading all the more implausible. The more plausible reading of the passage is provided as soon as we see that *prove* is to be understood in the sense of "prove to be." Since we know that the works of God are formed by boundless love and wisdom, this dark state, this infancy of being, cannot *prove (to be)* its final issue. What is consoling then is the knowledge that the human spirit must progress, and this consolation—a much more consoling one than Cohen's—is allowed us precisely because of what we do know about God's nature.

38. Lovejoy, *The Great Chain of Being,* passim.

39. Cf., however, *Winter,* 572–86, which suggests the possibility of our coming to know the order of harmony in this life.

40. The notion of a chain of being made of types of things classified by the reason may help to explain one of the most prominent—and, for most modern readers, annoying—stylistic features of the poem, namely, the use of compound epithets and two-word periphrases such as "liquid air" and "scaly kind." If reason divides things into classes, then these classes may be identified in terms of their differentia, namely, the defining characteristics that distinguish species from one another. Thus, just as man is a rational animal, fish are the scaly kind. Cf. John Arthos, *The Language of Natural Description in Eighteenth-Century Poetry* (Ann Arbor: University of Michigan Press, 1949), pp. 17, 230.

41. For histories of the sublime and its theories and conventions, see Marjorie Hope Nicolson, *Mountain Gloom and Mountain Glory: The Development of the Aesthetics of the Infinite* (Ithaca: Cornell University Press, 1959); and Samuel Holt Monk, *The Sublime: A Study of Critical Theories in XVIII-Century England* (1935; reprint, Ann Arbor: University of Michigan Press, 1960).

42. Edmund Burke, *A Philosophical Enquiry into the Origin of Our Ideas of the Sublime and Beautiful,* ed. J. T. Boulton (London: Routledge, 1958), p. 62.

43. Cf. *Summer,* 456–66 in the first edition (James Thomson, *The Seasons,* ed. James Sambrook [Oxford: Clarendon Press, 1981], pp. 281–82), where the sublimity is weaker and the language of degrees absent.

44. Cf. Richard Hönigswald's comments on the relationship between biblical Chaos and biblical Order, in *Vom erkenntnistheoretischen Gehalt alter Schöpfungserzählungen, Richard Hönigswald: Schriften aus dem Nachlass,* no. 1 (Stuttgart: Kohlhammer, 1957), p. 168: "Ein tiefer erkenntnistheoretischer Sinn verbirgt sich so hinter dem Gedanken, daß auch das Chaos göttliches Schöpfungswerk sei. Denn in ihm erfährt der dialektische Zwiespalt zwischen einem grundsätzlich ordnungsjenseitigen Chaos und dem überschaubar gefügten Kosmos seine grundsätzliche Überwindung. Nun erscheint das Chaos nicht mehr—man erinnere sich der einschlägigen Bemerkungen zum babylonischen Schöpfungsmythos—als ein inkonsequentermaßen außerhalb jedes Bereichs der Bestimmtheit verharrendes und in unfaßbarer Gestaltung zum Kosmos hin begriffenes οὐκ ὄν; nun ist es nach demselben Prinzip, nämlich nach der Idee des 'Anfangs,' gesetzt, das die kosmogonische Bestimmtheit der Natur beherrscht. Nun bietet sich das Chaos in unveräußer-

licher Kontinuität zur Natur also deren μὴ ὄν dar. Nun tritt an die Stelle jener pseudodialek-
tischen Kluft zwischen Chaos und Kosmos ein dialektisch-fruchtbarer Ansatz: Im Chaos
ergreift die biblische Schöpfungsgeschichte nicht nur tatsächlich, sondern prinzipiell die
Bestimmtheit der Natur—immer freilich im Sinne eines Inbegriffs aller Ereignisse, d.h. der
spezifischen, metaphysisch-eschatologischen Gegebenheit der Welt, immer aber auch nach
Maßgabe des einzigartigen Systems von Bedingungen, die den kosmogonischen Begriff des
'Anfangs' ausmachen. Nun erst gelangen Chaos und Relativität des Chaos zu definierbaren
Funktionen."

5

Encyclopedic Form:
The Triumph of the Arbitrary

And though one says that one is part of everything,

There is a conflict, there is a resistance involved;
And being part is an exertion that declines:
      —Wallace Stevens, "The Course of a Particular"

Editorial Authority and the Ascription of Meaning

The preceding three chapters have indicated some of the ways in which seventeenth- and eighteenth-century writers used open forms to represent views concerning the structure of knowledge or the structure of reality. And since I disclaim any ambition to provide either a comprehensive taxonomy of open forms or a history of the open form during the seventeenth and eighteenth centuries, it might seem that the choice of which examples to discuss, or how many, necessarily becomes an arbitrary one. However, although I shall not presume to argue that my choice or arrangement of texts reflects any ineluctable logic, or that the texts to be discussed in this chapter have any irrefragable claim to provide the perfect capstone to this study, I fear that, despite all my diffidence, some such conclusions may suggest themselves in the course of what follows. The reasons for this, I think, lie both in the special relationships that obtain between the two encyclopedias to be discussed here and the works that have been discussed in previous chapters, and, above all, in the special nature of these encyclopedias as limiting cases for the representational capacity of open forms.

But before we can examine those characteristics which render our encyclopedic texts uniquely suitable for treatment here, we need to consider those features of encyclopedias in general that may seem to render them, at first glance, particularly *dubious* choices for inclusion. I am thinking of those features which would seem to militate against the ascription of representational significance to the forms of encyclopedias.

First there is the fact that the basic form of any encyclopedia is normally dictated by convention and by considerations of convenience and necessity. Indeed, the *Discours préliminaire* to Diderot's *Encyclopédie* justifies the alphabetical arrangement first on the basis of its convenience for the reader:

> Il nous a paru plus commode et plus facile pour nos lecteurs, qui désirant de s'instruire sur la signification d'un mot, le trouveront plus aisément dans un Dictionnaire alphabétique que dans tout autre.

> We thought it would be more convenient for our readers: wishing to learn about the meaning of a word, they would be able to find it more easily in an alphabetical dictionary than in any other kind,

and second on the basis of the difficulties that other forms would have entailed in the matter of pooling the talents of several authors:

> D'ailleurs, s'il eût été question de faire de chaque science ou de chaque art un traité particulier dans la forme ordinaire, et de réunir seulement ces différents traités sous le titre d'Encyclopédie, il eut été bien plus difficile de rassembler pour cet ouvrage un si grand nombre de personnes, et la plupart de nos collègues auraient sans doute mieux aimé donner séparément leur ouvrage, que de le voir confondu avec un grand nombre d'autres.

> Furthermore, if the project had been to produce, in the conventional form, a separate treatise on each art and each science, and simply to put these treatises together under the title of *Encyclopedia,* it would have been more difficult to assemble so many collaborators, and most of our colleagues would no doubt have preferred having their contributions presented separately to seeing them merged with many others.

Then there is the fact that the editors were bound by certain commitments:

> De plus, en suivant ce dernier plan, [that of collecting a series of separate treatises] nous eussions été forcés de renoncer presque entièrement à l'usage que nous voulions faire de l'Encyclopédie angloise [Chambers's *Cyclopaedia*] entraînés tant par la réputation de cet Ouvrage, que par l'Ancien *Prospectus,* approuvé du Public, & auquel nous

désirions de nous conformer. La Traduction entière de cette Encyclopédie nous a été remise entre les mains par les libraires qui avoient
entrepris de la publier; nous l'avons distribuée à nos Collegues, qui ont
mieux aimé se charger de la revoir, de la corriger, et de l'augmenter que
de s'engager sans avoir, pour ainsi dire, aucun matériaux pré-
paratoires. . . . D'un autre côté, quelques-uns de ces Savans, en posses-
sion de leur Partie long-tems avant que nous fussions Editeurs,
l'avoient déjà fort avancée en suivant l'ancien projet de l'ordre alphabétique; il nous eût par conséquent été impossible de changer ce
projet quand-même nous aurions été moins disposé à l'approuver.

In addition, following this plan [that of collecting a series of separate
treatises] would have kept us from making use of the English encyclopedia [Chambers's *Cyclopaedia*], a course to which we were committed both because of the reputation of that work, and because we
wished to adhere to the original *Prospectus,* which had won the ap-
proval of the public. The booksellers who had originally undertaken to
publish that encyclopedia provided us with the complete translation,
which we, in turn, distributed among our colleagues; they preferred
revising, correcting, and augmenting it, to engaging themselves without, so to speak, preliminary materials. . . . On the other hand, some
of these scholars, having been given their assignments long before we
became editors, had already made substantial progress on them, in
accordance with the original plan of an alphabetical arrangement. As a
consequence, it would have been impossible to change this plan even if
we had been less inclined to endorse it.

Finally, after adding to these arguments the somewhat lame assertion that the alphabetical arrangement did not seem to have
caused Chambers "aucunes difficultés," the justification closes
with what seems to be a classic case of making a virtue of necessity:

Tout se réunissoit donc pour nous obliger de rendre cet Ouvrage con-
forme à un plan que nous aurions suivi par choix, si nous en eussions
été les maîtres.[1]

Thus everything combined to oblige us to have this work conform to a
plan which, if it had been up to us, we would have followed by choice.

Now, despite the appeals to convenience and convention, the
very existence of such a justification alerts us to the fact that the use
of an alphabetical format is not being viewed simply as a given of
encyclopedia-making. For one does not justify one course of action unless one can imagine being reproached for not having fol-

lowed another. And indeed I shall show not only that both Chambers and Diderot thought that they would deserve reproach if their great collections of knowledge were not organized in such a way as to reflect the overall structure of that knowledge, but that both editors actually justified the forms of their encyclopedias precisely on the ground that they performed such a representational function.

Those justifications are the focal point of this chapter, but before looking at them we need to consider how they can be squared with the fact—duly acknowledged, as we have just seen, in the case of the *Encyclopédie*—that the form of an encyclopedia is dictated by considerations of convenience and necessity. The forms of the other works that we have examined, moreover, were devised or adapted by their authors, who fashioned them precisely for their representational significance. But neither Chambers nor Diderot was the sole author of his encyclopedia, and Diderot was not even the sole editor of his. And although Chambers does not offer a counterpart of the acknowledgment, in the *Discours préliminaire*, of the constraints that impinged on the form of the *Encyclopédie*, it is easy to imagine that some such constraints were in fact at work. How then can the form of these encyclopedias be endowed with representational meaning?

Although the answer to this question follows straightforwardly from the principles established in chapter 1, I think that it is worth making this answer explicit, however sketchily, before I proceed to the main business of this chapter. First, even if we assume that neither Diderot nor Chambers could have chosen anything other than an alphabetical format for their encyclopedias, they did have some leeway in their approaches to and use of this format. For the final form of each encyclopedia, rather than being strictly a function of the alphabetical arrangement, is, as we shall see, partly determined by other relationships between the articles, including those established by means of cross-references. These relationships, which will figure prominently in my discussion of the forms of the two encyclopedias, are of course relevant to the question of how the forms of encyclopedias are endowed with meaning. But even if the editors of the encyclopedias had in no way altered or acted upon a conventional alphabetical format, they nonetheless had the capacity to endow the forms of their encyclopedias with meaning. It will be recalled that the resemblance between an open form and its object is never sufficiently specific to establish, by itself, the representational function of that form. The same form can resemble any number of things, and the determination that a given resemblance is operative depends upon a judgment as to the intentions of the author. It follows that the meaning of a form is not simply a function of anything intrinsic in that form, and that the same form can have different meanings in the hands of different authors. The author provides a form with meaning not necessarily by putting something into that form, but rather by assigning a meaning to it. This being the case, the fact that the author normally both makes the form and assigns meaning to it in no way entails that the making of the form and the assignment of meaning are one and the same activity. They may be, on the contrary, two distinct activities.

The author's power to determine meaning, of course, is a privilege that we conventionally grant him, but it is a privilege that the author must not abuse. The ascription of meaning must be consistent with the resemblances that actually obtain between the form and its object, and with the resemblances to other forms that constitute a representational convention.[2] Thus a discontinuous form may represent one of several possible things, and the author may choose from among these. But the form cannot represent just anything—no matter what the author says or does.

Since the meaning of a form is ascribed to it, within the bounds allowed by resemblance and convention, there is no reason, in principle, why the meaning could not be ascribed just as easily by an editor as by an author. Certainly, if Francis Bacon had not written the *Novum Organum,* but had edited it in such a way as to turn it into an aphoristic work, that is, by breaking it up into typographically distinct parts and numbering those parts, while retaining grammatical transitions between them, then we would feel no need to revise the judgment made in chapter 2 as to the meaning of the work's form. But we should be obliged to acknowledge that in interpreting the meaning of the form, we were interpreting, not the intentions of the authors, but those of the editor.

Now, in the case of Bacon's hypothetical edition of the *Novum Organum,* the editor is not simply ascribing meaning to the form, but is also doing something to it: he is acting upon it, changing it. And indeed, it would be this activity that alerted us to the editor's consciousness of form and that suggested that he was endowing the form with meaning. But we can be alerted to the meaning of a form in other ways. The real Francis Bacon, after all, indicated his intentions, not by creating the aphoristic format, but by explicitly dis-

cussing the representational capacities of the traditional format that
he had adopted. And if an author, by means of such a discussion,
can ascribe meaning to a form that he has merely inherited, an
editor can surely do the same thing. Both Chambers and Diderot,
in fact, do explicitly discuss the relationships between the forms of
their encyclopedias and certain ideas that those forms resemble (or
embody), and this, independently of the fact that they also determined the overall forms into which the alphabetical arrangement
was incorporated, would be sufficient to justify my claim that each
of them endows his encyclopedic form with meaning.

Buffon and the Imaginary Encyclopedia of Particulars

Before we turn at last to the works of Chambers and Diderot
themselves, it will be useful to glance at a text that, although it can
have influenced only one of our encyclopedists, will facilitate our
understanding of both. Buffon's *Histoire naturelle* (with substantial contributions by Daubenton) appeared in 1749, twenty-one
years after the first edition of Chambers's *Cyclopaedia* and a few
months before the appearance of Diderot's *Prospectus* to the forth-
coming *Encyclopédie*. In the *Premier discours: De la manière
d'étudier et de traiter l'histoire naturelle*, Buffon formulates his
famous attack on Linnaeus's still more famous classifications of
plants and animals. Buffon's principal complaint against Linnaeus
centered not so much on the classifications themselves as on their
purported relationship to external reality. Linnaeus seemed to
think that the divisions of animals and plants into species, genera,
and classes were natural ones, that they were based on real essences
shared by the members of each group, and that all that had been
necessary had been to "discover" these groupings. But Buffon
replied that placing individuals into distinct classes falsifies nature,
which "marche par des gradations inconnues" and which passes
from species to species, from genus to genus "par des nuances
imperceptibles."[3] Of course, to see nature as eluding classification
because classes, rather than being distinct, actually shade off into
one another, is to imply that every classificatory demarcation arbitrarily imposes itself between distinct individuals, and that nature
is really made up not of classes but of individuals. And this is
precisely the conclusion that Buffon reaches:

> Plus on augmentera le nombre des divisions des productions na-
> turelles, plus on approchera du vrai, puisqu'il n'existe réellement dans

la nature que des individus, et que les genres, les ordres, les classes n'existent que dans notre imagination.[4]

The more one increases the number of divisions of the products of nature, the closer one approaches to the truth. For in nature, the only things that really exist are individuals; genera, orders, and classes exist only in our imagination.

This is not to say, however, that grouping plants and animals according to certain shared characteristics is pointless:

En effet, ce ne sont que des rapports arbitraires & des points de vûe différens sous lesquels on a considéré les objets de la Nature, & en ne faisant usage des méthodes [i.e., classifications] que dans cet esprit, on peut en tirer quelqu'utilité; car quoique cela ne paroisse pas fort néces-saire, cependant il pourroit être bon qu'on sçût toutes les espèces de plantes dont les feuilles se ressemblent, toutes celles dont les fleurs sont semblables, toutes celles qui nourrissent de certaines espèces d'in-sectes, toutes celles qui ont un certain nombre d'étamines, toutes celles qui ont de certaines glandes excrétoires; & de même dans les animaux, tous ceux qui ont un certain nombre de doigts.[5]

In fact, the objects of nature have been considered according to arbi-trary resemblances and varying points of view, but if classifications are employed without losing sight of this fact, they can be useful; for although it does not appear to be necessary, it could be valuable to know all the species of plants whose leaves resemble one another, all those with similar flowers, all those which provide nourishment to certain species of insects, all those with a certain number of stamens, all those with certain excretory glands; and likewise, among animals, all those with a certain number of digits.

In going on to explain just what it is that endows these arbitrary groupings with "quelqu'utilité," Buffon employs a metaphor that is of more than passing interest in our present context:

Chacune de ces méthodes n'est, à parler vrai, qu'un Dictionnaire où l'on trouve les noms rangez dans un ordre relatif à cette idée, & par conséquent aussi arbitraire que l'ordre alphabétique; mais l'avantage qu'on en pourroit tirer, c'est qu'en comparant tous ces résultats, on se retrouveroit enfin à la vraie méthode, qui est la description complète & l'histoire exacte de chaque chose en particulier.[6]

Each of these classifications is, correctly understood, nothing but a dictionary in which one finds the headings arranged with respect to this or that idea, and consequently as arbitrary as an alphabetical arrangement; but the profit that one can derive from these [arbitrary arrangements] is that in comparing all these results, one will finally come upon the *true* method, which is the complete description and exact history of each thing in particular.

Grouping animals or plants according to some point of resemblance or other is, for Buffon, an arbitrary procedure, like grouping words alphabetically in a dictionary. The principal virtue of these classifications is precisely to reveal, by dint of their very plurality, their own essential artificiality. This artificiality, in turn, points to the fact that it is only the individuals themselves, and not their arbitrary groupings, that deserve our studious attention.

The procedure that Buffon describes, according to which systematic arrangements serve merely to undermine themselves, to reveal their affinity with the artificial arrangements of dictionaries, is, of course, rather a roundabout one. One could imagine indicating the particularity of things by presenting them in an arrangement that is *prima facie* arbitrary, that is, in the alphabetical arrangement of a dictionary or encyclopedia. Such a procedure, in its absolute form, would reverse Buffon's metaphor and collapse its poles. If classifications based on resemblance are arbitrary and hence like the arrangements of encyclopedias, then an "ideal" encyclopedia would not merely describe the constituents of our knowledge, but embody their contingent structure (assuming that Buffon's nominalism applied not only to plants and animals, but to reality in general) in its structure. The form of such an encyclopedia would represent both reality and the encyclopedia's own discursive representation of reality; thus form would become a metaphor for itself.

Such an encyclopedia of particulars, of course, does not exist. The articles of a real encyclopedia, such as Chambers's *Cyclopaedia*, do not, as a rule, have for their subject matters such particulars as an individual tree or a particular fish. Rather, their articles treat mostly phenomena that are indicated by common nouns. These articles group things together, swallowing up their particularity. A diligent encyclopedist then, would be hard pressed utterly to collapse Buffon's metaphor, but he could at least reverse it. If the arrangement of phenomena into an allegedly ordered system is really like the arbitrary arrangement of an encyclopedia, then the arbitrary structure of an encyclopedia is like the structure of reality, and hence can represent this structure. Chambers, as we shall now see, performed just such an inversion of Buffon's metaphor, albeit *ante rem*, and in so doing established the representational function of his encyclopedic form.

Ephraim Chambers and the Lockean Encyclopedia of Particulars

The first thing that Ephraim Chambers announces in the Preface to his *Cyclopaedia* (1728) is that he has striven to give the work a structure beyond that of a mere haphazard assemblage of articles: "The difficulty lay in the form, and economy of it; so to dispose such a multitude of materials, as not to make a confused heap of incoherent Parts, but one consistent Whole." "And here it must be confessed," Chambers goes on to complain, "there was little assistance to be had." Former encyclopedists

> have scarce attempted anything like a structure in their works; nor seem to have been aware, that a dictionary was, in some measure capable of the advantages of a continued discourse. Hence it is, that we see nothing like a whole in what they have done: and, for this reason, such materials as they did afford for the present work, generally needed farther preparation, ere they became fit for our purpose; which was as different from most of theirs, as a system from a cento.[7]

Chambers thus considered his function to include that of providing a structure for his work, to turn its disparate parts into a consistent whole. But to organize the parts of an encyclopedia into a whole is more than a merely aesthetic endeavor; for to give a structure to the parts of an encyclopedia is to give a structure to human knowledge itself. This Chambers proposed to do by means of cross-references:

> Our view was, to consider the several matters, not only in themselves, but relatively, as they respect each other; both to treat them as so many wholes, and as so many parts of some greater whole; their connexion with which to be pointed out by a reference. So that by a course of references, from generals to particulars; from premises, to conclusions; from cause, to effect, and vice versa, *i.e.* from more, to less complex, and from less, to more; a communication might be opened between the several parts of the work; and the several articles be, in some measure, replaced in their natural order of science, out of which the alphabetical order had removed them.[8]

Thus the form of the *Cyclopaedia* will transcend the alphabetical arrangement without discarding it, will make a whole out of parts without losing sight of the parts. And having already encountered, in Thomson's *Seasons,* the traditional notion that discrete parts are a necessary precondition for an orderly whole, we should be quick to recognize the presuppositions that Chambers is invoking here. And indeed, Chambers soon goes on explicitly to defend the retention of the alphabetical arrangement in a manner that more strongly recalls the notion that a whole without parts is not an orderly whole:

> It may be even said, that if the System be an improvement upon the Dictionary; the Dictionary is some advantage to the System; and that this is, perhaps, the only way wherein the whole circle, or body of knowledge, with all its parts and dependences, can well be delivered. In any other form, many thousand lesser things must needs be concealed: all the pins, the joints, the binding of the fabric, must be invisible of course; all the lesser parts, one might say, all the parts whatsoever, must be, in some measure swallowed in the whole. The imagination, stretched and amplified to take in so large a structure, can have but a very general, undistinguishing perception of any of the component parts.—Whereas the parts are not less matter of knowledge when taken separately, than when put together.[9]

This claim that the alphabetical format of the encyclopedia keeps the parts of knowledge from being swallowed up by the whole is certainly convincing, but it convinces at the expense of Chambers's other claim, that the disparate parts are to be welded into a systematic whole. For while one may easily imagine systematic presentations of knowledge that use conventional internal divisions— such as chapters, sections, and subsections—to keep track of the parts without taking anything away from the structure of the whole, the alphabetical arrangement—no matter how numerous the cross-references—would seem to give primacy to the parts at the expense of the whole. This tilt away from unity is, in fact, intensified by a second justification of the alphabetical arrangement, one that places even stronger valuation on the parts of knowledge. This second justification, moreover, while claiming to be a mere confirmation of the first, actually provides a much more forceful and precise justification of the *Cyclopaedia*'s form, and, in so doing, reveals its representational function:

> Nay, and as our ideas are all individuals; and as every thing that exists is one, it may seem more natural to consider knowledge in its parts, *i.e.*

as divided into separate articles, denoted by so many different terms; than to consider the whole assemblage in its utmost composition; which is a thing merely artificial and the work of imagination.[10]

In this passage Chambers is invoking the tremendously influential epistemological theories of John Locke. For Locke, a complex idea, such as that of a given man or tree, is composed by an act of the mind out of the simple ideas of qualities (shape, color, solidity) that are the fundamental givens of experience and the building blocks of our conceptual universe.[11] More abstract ideas, such as those of men in general or trees in general, are similarly products of the human mind rather than features of external reality:

> [G]*eneral* and *universal* belong not to the real existence of things, but *are the inventions* and *creatures of the understanding*, made by it for its own use, and *concern only signs*, whether words or *ideas.* Words are general . . . when used for signs of general *ideas*, and so are applicable indifferently to many particular things: but universality belongs not to things themselves, which are all of them particular in their existence. . . . When therefore we quit particulars, the generals that rest are only creatures of our own making: their general nature being nothing but the capacity they are put into, by the understanding, of signifying or representing many particulars.[12]

Locke's rejection of universals, or real essences, is part of a general trend of seventeenth- and eighteenth-century philosophy, and Buffon's views on classification represent nothing more than an application of this general philosophical attitude[13] to the field of natural history. (That Chambers's own application of this view to his conception of encyclopedic form is specifically Lockean in inspiration is indicated by the fact that he refers to the particularity of our *ideas* of things. It was Locke who began the empiricist tradition of approaching the issue through a genetic analysis of the contents of human consciousness, namely, ideas.)

Chambers's second, Lockean, justification of the alphabetical arrangement is in accord with the first, more traditional, one insofar as both ascribe positive value to distinct parts. But the Lockean justification enables us to understand the relationship between Chambers's valuation of the parts and his claims about the unifying function of the cross-references. On the one hand, since complex ideas are inventions of the human mind, there is no necessary correspondence between them and external reality; and, of course, this extends to our more general complex ideas, those which classify the objects of our experience into species or kinds. One contemporary philosopher characterizes Locke's results thus:

> If . . .[man] is to think of [the external world] in general terms at all, that is to say, if he is not to be limited to statements about particular observations, he has to frame concepts. But he can never then be sure that what he is thinking about has anything corresponding to it in the real world.[14]

But if our complex ideas do not provide knowledge about any complex counterparts in the external world, that does not mean that they provide us with no knowledge at all. For Locke defines knowledge in such a way as to place value on what we can ascertain about the ideas themselves and their relationship to one another:

> *All our complex* ideas, *except those of substances,* being *archetypes* of the mind's own making, not intended to be the copies of anything nor referred to the existence of anything as to their originals, *cannot want any conformity necessary to real knowledge.* For that which is not designed to represent anything but itself can never be capable of a wrong representation nor mislead us from the true apprehension of anything by its dislikeness to it; and such, excepting those of substances, are all our complex *ideas.* Which, as I have shown in another place, are combinations of ideas which the mind, by its free choice, puts together, without considering any connexion they have in nature.[15]

Locke's sensationalist epistemology thus seems to place its primary valuation on parts rather than wholes—on simple ideas as opposed to complex ones, and on the ideas of particulars as opposed to those of universals. For in each opposition, the individual part conforms most closely to external reality, to the real mode of existence of things. On the other hand, the combinations of simple ideas that comprise complex ones, and the general ideas by which we group particulars can, once their limitations vis-à-vis external reality are recognized, provide real knowledge. Chambers's invocation of this Lockean relationship between part and whole in his justification for the encyclopedic form establishes the resemblance between Locke's view of the microstructure of knowledge, at the level of simple and complex ideas, particulars and universals, and the *Cyclopaedia's* organization of the macrostructure of human knowledge. Because of Locke's discovery that "our own ideas are all individuals" and that "everything that exists is one," it is "more natural to consider knowledge in its parts, i.e. as divided into separate articles . . . than to consider the whole assemblage in its utmost composition, which is a thing merely artificial and the work of imagination."

The form of the *Cyclopaedia* thus represents the microstructure of human knowledge as described in some of the major tenets of Lockean theory. But Chambers is also implying that the same Lockean principles that give primacy to parts at the level of the microstructure also operate at the level of the macrostructure. In fact, later in the Preface Chambers observes that the sciences themselves and their interconnections are mere artificial constructs and the products of historical contingency:

> [T]his distribution of the land of science, like that of the face of the earth and heavens, is wholly arbitrary; and might be altered, perhaps not without advantage. Had not Alexander, Caesar, and Gengiskan lived, the division of the terraqueous globe had, doubtless, been very different from what we now find it: and the case would have been the same with the world of learning, had no such person been born as Aristotle.

These divisions of knowledge hamper progress, and in an observation that strikingly anticipates more recent interdisciplinary manifestos, Chambers considers the advantages of ignoring these arbitrary disciplinary boundaries:

> I do not know whether it might not be more for the general interest of learning, to have the partitions thrown down, and the whole laid in common again. . . . Our inquiries, in such case, would not be confined to so narrow bounds; but we should be led to explore many a rich tract, now doomed to lie neglected because without the pale.[16]

Buffon, as we have seen, suggested that the virtue of various conflicting classifications was to reveal their arbitrariness and to direct our attention to the individuals themselves. Chambers thinks that all the branches of learning are arbitrary groupings of parts of knowledge. But rather than presenting the parts in systematic groupings that ignore their own arbitrariness, he presents them as parts, in separate articles whose alphabetical arrangement emphasizes their separateness. But this is not to say that Chambers, like Buffon, ultimately places value exclusively on the parts. Like Locke, and probably more strongly than Locke, he has faith in the value of the connections between the parts. This faith is attested to by his multifarious cross-references. But even while indicating that real knowledge may be obtained by connecting the parts, the cross-references reflect the view that the parts of our knowledge may be connected in various ways, and that these connections are not features of the world, but works of the imagination—whether that of the scholar, or the scientist, or the encyclopedist.

The relationship between the form of the *Cyclopaedia* and Locke's sensationalist epistemology is ultimately a reciprocal one. The form of the work represents the microstructure of knowledge, as described by Locke, but this microstructure also informs the macrostructure of knowledge as presented by the encyclopedia. Thus, although Chambers's work is not an encyclopedia of particulars, it is an encyclopedia whose form represents both the primacy of particulars (and of simple ideas), and the primacy of parts in the larger structure of human knowledge.

The Dialogue of the *Encyclopédie*

Diderot's most extended and interesting discussion of the general structure of the *Encyclopédie* is to be found in the article "Encyclopédie," which appeared in its proper alphabetical place in the fifth volume. After claiming that there are as many ways to organize encyclopedic knowledge as there are ways for an "architecte du génie le plus féconde" to design a large building, Diderot goes on to consider some of the possibilities that were available to him:

> Il [l'ordre encyclopédique] peut être formé, soit en rapportant nos différéntes connaissances aux diverses facultés de notre âme . . . soit en les rapportant aux êtres, qu'elles ont pour objet; et cet objet est ou de pure curiosité, ou de luxe, ou de nécessité. On peut diviser la science générale, ou en science des choses et en science des signes, ou en science des concrets, ou en science des abstraits. Les deux causes les plus générales, l'art et la nature, donnent aussi une belle et grande distribution. On en rencontrera d'autres dans la distinction ou du physique et du moral, de l'existant et du possible, du matériel et du spirituel, du réel et de l'intelligible. Tout ce que nous savons ne découle-t-il pas de l'usage de nos sens et de celui de notre raison? n'est-il pas ou naturel, ou révélé? ne sont-ce pas ou des mots, ou des choses, ou des faits?[17]

It could be structured either according to the correspondence between the various branches of knowledge and the diverse faculties of our souls, or their correspondence to the beings that they have for their object; whether the object be considered out of idle curiosity, or because of its superfluity, or its necessity. One could divide universal knowledge either into the science of things and that of signs, or that of concrete things and that of abstractions. The two most general causes, art and nature, also provide a beautiful and grand arrangement. One will find other arrangements in the distinction between the physical and the moral, that between the existent and the possible, that between the real and the intelligible. Does not everything we know derive from our senses and our reason? Is it not natural or revealed knowledge, knowledge of words, or of things, or of facts?

This multiplicity of possibilities, Diderot goes on to say, in a passage indebted to Buffon, is a function of the fact that the universe is made up of particulars that have no order of their own:

Il est donc impossible de bannir l'arbitraire de cette grande distribution première. L'univers ne nous offre que des êtres particuliers, infinis en nombre, et sans presque aucune division fixe et déterminée; il n'y en a aucun qu'on puisse appeler ou le premier ou le dernier; tout s'y enchaîne et s'y succède par des nuances insensibles; et à travers cette uniforme immensité d'objets, s'il en paraît quelques-uns qui, comme des pointes de rochers, semblent percer la surface et la dominer, ils ne doivent cette prérogative qu'à des systèmes particuliers, qu'à des conventions vagues, qu'à certains événements étrangers, et non à l'arrangement physique des êtres et à l'intention de la nature.[18]

It is thus impossible to exclude the arbitrary from this first great arrangement. The universe presents us only with individual beings, infinite in number, and virtually without any fixed or determinate boundaries; none of these particular beings can be identified as the first or the last; they are all linked, and one gives way to the next imperceptibly; and if across the uniform immensity of objects, there are some which, like crags, seem to pierce the surface and dominate it, they owe their preeminence merely to particular systems, to certain vague conventions, to certain obscure events, and not to the physical order of things or to the intentions of nature.

Diderot here is not considering the various principles of organization that might replace the alphabetical arrangement, but rather the principles by which the knowledge being displayed in alphabetically arranged articles might be organized so as to indicate the underlying connections between the distinct parts of knowledge. And these connections, as in the case of Chambers's *Cyclopaedia*, will be indicated by means of unifying cross-references. In the

light of our consideration of Chambers and Buffon, we might well
be tempted to read Diderot's declaration of the arbitrariness of the
various orderings of knowledge as an indication that the alphabetical arrangement itself is an image of the stubborn particularity of
things, and that the cross-references are a representation of a coun-
tervailing impulse toward unification. But although such a tension
between anti-essentialism and organization, inherited from Chambers and buttressed by Buffon, is clearly at work in the *Encyclopédie,* there is an additional factor that needs to enter into our
interpretation of Diderot's encyclopedic structure, namely, the relationships between the editor and the work of his various authors,
the "Société des hommes de lettres."

Diderot's discussion of these relationships emerges from his discussion of the general scheme of knowledge that is presumably
reflected in the assignment of articles, the designation of the discipline to which each article belongs, and the cross-references that
connect the articles to one another. For despite Diderot's acknowledgment that all attempts to classify human knowledge are arbitrary, a general scheme of knowledge has, in fact, been adopted for
the *Encyclopédie,*[19] and the choice, paradoxically, has not been an
altogether arbitrary one. It is, in fact, in the context of a
justification of this scheme of knowledge that Diderot's discussion
of the arbitrariness of such schemes is situated.

The "official" scheme of knowledge enshrined in the *Encyclopédie,* derived from Bacon and presented in the form of a dia-
gram (the "Système figuré des connoissances humaines" that appeared both in the *Prospectus* and in the first volume), is one
according to which the branches of knowledge arise from the main
faculties of the human mind: memory, reason, and imagination.
History, in its various branches, sacred, political, and natural, is a
function of memory; philosophy and science, in their various
branches, are functions of reason; and the fine arts are functions of
imagination. Diderot's justification for choosing such a scheme is
an eloquently humanistic one:

> Une considération surtout qu'il ne faut point perdre de vue, c'est
> que si l'on bannit l'homme ou l'être pensant et contemplateur de dessus
> la surface de la terre, ce spectacle pathétique et sublime de la nature
> n'est plus qu'une scène triste et muette; l'univers se tait, le silence et la
> nuit s'en emparent. Tout se change en une vaste solitude où les
> phénomènes inobservés se passent d'une manière obscure et sourde.
> C'est la présence de l'homme qui rend l'existence des êtres intéressante:
> et que peut-on se proposer de mieux dans l'histoire de ces êtres que de

se soumettre à cette considération? Pourquoi n'introduirons-nous pas l'homme dans notre ouvrage, comme il est placé dans l'univers? Pourquoi n'en ferons-nous pas un centre commun? Est-il, dans l'espace infini, quelque point d'où nous puissions, avec plus d'avantage, faire partir les lignes immenses que nous proposons d'étendre à tous les autres points? (P. 453)

One paramount consideration which must not be lost sight of, is that if one excludes man, the thinking and contemplative being, from the surface of the earth, this moving and sublime drama of nature becomes nothing more than a mute and sorrowful stage. The world becomes still, consumed by silence and the night. Everything changes into a vast solitude where the unobserved phenomena are dark and muffled. It is the presence of man than renders the existence of objects interesting: and in presenting the history of these objects, how can one do better than to yield to this consideration? Why not give man a place in our work, like the place that he occupies in the world? Why not make him our common center? Is there, in the infinity of space, a better point from which to radiate the great lines with which we propose to reach all the other points?

It is this consideration, Diderot concludes, that has led him "à chercher dans les facultés principales de l'homme la division générale à laquelle nous avons subordonné notre travail." Although there are "une infinité de points de vue" according to which the universe might be represented (p. 451), the one he has chosen may be said to represent the point of view of the human race in general.

Diderot, of course, does not have the temerity to claim that the scheme of knowledge that he has chosen is the *only* one that may be said to reflect the perspective of mankind. In fact, he seems to acknowledge that even the establishment of his humanistic criterion, while it would exclude some rival schemes of knowledge, would allow others beyond the one chosen for the *Encyclopédie:*

Qu'on suive telle autre voie qu'on aimera mieux, pourvu qu'on ne substitue pas à l'homme un être muet, insensible et froid. (P. 453)

Follow whatever other course you may prefer, provided that you do not replace man with an object that is mute, insensible, and cold.

Thus, although Diderot's rhetoric tends to justify his adopted scheme, he acknowledges that his reasoning does not altogether free the choice from the taint of the arbitrary.

The significance of all this for our reading of the form of the

Encyclopédie cannot be ascertained until we pass from Diderot's discussion of the *ordre général* to his subsequent discussion of the other "orders" of the work.

A second order, no less essential than the one just discussed, Diderot tells us, is that which determines "l'étendue relative des différentes parties de l'ouvrage" (p. 453). The difficulty here is not simply that the size of the task militates against "une juste proportion entre les différentes parties," but, more significantly, that the *Encyclopédie* is the product of many hands:

> Quand ce tout serait l'ouvrage d'un seul homme, la tâche ne serait pas facile; qu'est-ce donc que cette tâche, lorsque le tout est l'ouvrage d'une société nombreuse? (P. 454)

> Even if this were the work of a single man, the task would not be easy; what must the task be like when the whole thing is the work of numerous collaborators?

The multiplicity of scholars contributing to the work means that there is a multiplicity of limited perspectives: "Chacun a sa manière de sentir et de voir." Moreover, there is a spirit of competition among the contributors, which results in the disproportionate inflation of articles:

> l'émulation qui s'allume nécessairement entre des collègues produit des dissertations au lieu d'articles. (P. 455–56)

> the rivalry which, as a matter of course, flares up between some colleagues, gives rise to dissertations instead of articles.

The result of these clashes of individual perspective is the reign of disorder (p. 456). In fact, when looked at from a literary point of view, the form of the *Encyclopédie* is, at best, a monstrosity: "vous comparerez l'ouvrage entier au monstre de l'*Art poétique*, ou même à quelque chose de plus hideux" (p. 455). But this monstrous disproportion will gradually disappear in subsequent editions,

> lorsque le temps aura pressé les connaissances, et réduit chaque sujet à sa juste étendue. (P. 455)

> when time will have shaped knowledge, and reduced each subject to its proper dimension.

This prediction suggests that the chaotic form of the present *Encyclopédie* is a function not only of limited personal perspectives, but also of a limited temporal perspective, that of our present state of knowledge.

Beyond these personal and temporal perspectives, there are also more universal perspectives that, despite their universality, may contribute to the disproportionate form of the overall work. To the extent that subsequent editions fail to achieve a proper balance between the articles, it will be the result of the fact that some articles will have remained in their first-edition state because their subjects will have been neglected by science. And the blame for such neglect will fall on mankind in general, or on the French nation:

> S'il arrivait, après un grand nombre d'éditions successivement perfectionnées, que quelque matière importante restât dans le même état . . . ce ne sera plus la faute de l'ouvrage [i.e., the *Encyclopédie*], mais celle du genre humain en général, ou de la nation en particulier, dont les vues ne se seront pas encore tournées sur ces objets. (P. 455)

> If it happens, after several editions that are successively perfected, that some important material remains unchanged . . . it will not be the fault of the *Encyclopedia*, but that of humankind in general, or of the nation in particular, for not yet having turned its attention to these things.

This observation yields a paradoxical result: universally shared perspectives can, like conflicting personal perspectives, contribute to a disproportionate presentation of knowledge. Of course, this implicitly applies not only to future editions, but to the present edition as well. For if society's neglect of (or attentiveness toward) specific scientific topics can affect the structure of our knowledge as embodied in future editions, it must also have affected that structure in the present edition.

The *second ordre* of the *Encyclopédie* is thus a monstrously disproportionate one, whose disorder is a function of a complex clash of perspectives: the personal perspectives of the contributors, the perspective of the present moment with regard to the state of knowledge, and the perspective of society insofar as it determines how much attention is paid to developing the various branches of knowledge.

There remains a final, crucial perspective or, more precisely, a locus of perspectives, that impinges on the structure of the *Encyclopédie*, namely, that of the editor himself. The editor's role is first described in the discussion of the *quatrième ordre*,[20] "celui qui distribue convenablement plusieurs articles différents compris sous une même dénomination." The same word or term may belong to several arts or sciences, and something must be done to "former un petit système, dont l'objet principal soit d'adoucir et de pallier, autant qu'on pourra, la bizarrerie des disparates" (p. 457). Here the editor must take an active role, a role, in fact, akin to that of an author:

> Au milieu de ces différents articles de même dénomination à distribuer, l'éditeur se comportera comme s'il était l'auteur; il suivra l'ordre qu'il eût suivi, s'il eût eu à considérer le mot sous toutes ses acceptions. (P. 458)

> Attempting to arrange these varied articles that have the same heading, the editor will act as if he were the author; he will follow the order that he would have followed if he had had to consider the word in all of its meanings.

In ordering the disparate meanings of terms, the editor's skill and taste will stand him in good stead, but there are intractable forces that resist his attempts to impose order:

> Un bon esprit (et il faut supposer au moins cette qualité dans un éditeur) saura mettre chaque chose à sa place: et il n'y a pas à craindre qu'il ait dans les idées assez peu d'ordre, ou dans l'esprit assez peu de goût, pour entremêler, sans nécessité, des acceptions disparates; mais il y aurait aussi de l'injustice à l'accuser d'une bizarrerie qui ne serait que la suite nécessaire de la diversité des matières, des imperfections de la langue et de l'abus des métaphores, qui transporte un même mot de la boutique d'un artisan sur les bancs de la Sorbonne, et qui rassemble les choses les plus hétérogènes sous une commune dénomination. (P. 459)

> A good mind (and one has to suppose that an editor possesses nothing less) will know how to put each thing in its proper place; and there is no danger that his ideas will lack sufficient order, or that his mind will lack sufficient taste, to allow him to interweave disparate meanings—even when it is not necessary to do so; but it would also be unjust to blame him for an odd juxtaposition that was merely the necessary consequence of the diversity of subjects, of the imperfections of language, and of the abuse of metaphors, which carries the same word from a craftsman's shop to lecture halls of the Sorbonne, and which brings the most disparate things together under a common denomination.

In Diderot's other discussions of the arbitrariness of encyclopedic order, it was the lack of any inherent order in the external world, that is, the lack of real essences, that allowed for the imposition of various versions of order arising from a diversity of perspectives. But in attempting to order disparate meanings of the same words, the editor is confronted not with the passive acquiescence of the particulars in the universe, but with the stubborn arbitrariness already enshrined in language.[21]

The editor's perspective as embodied in the form of the *Encyclopédie* extends beyond his struggle to impose order on the *bizarreries* of language. It is, perhaps, most prominent, and certainly most complex, in the matter of the *renvois*.

Among Diderot's inheritances from Chambers was the notion that cross-references could counteract the fragmenting effect of arbitrarily arranged articles. Diderot describes this unifying function as follows:

Les renvois de choses éclaircissent l'objet, indiquent ses liaisons prochaines avec ceux qui le touchent immédiatement, et ses liaisons éloignées avec d'autres qu'on en croirait isolées, rappellent les notions communes et les principes analogues; fortifient les conséquences; entrelacent la branche au tronc, et donnent au tout cette unité si favorable à l'établissement de la vérité, et à la persuasion. (P. 462)

The "cross-references of things" illuminate the object, indicate its proximate relationship with those things that touch it immediately, and its more remote relationships with those other objects which one would suppose to be unconnected with it; they remind us of shared notions and analogous principles, reinforce the logical connections, link the branch to the trunk, and give to the whole that unity so conducive to the establishment of truth, and to persuasion.

However, although this passage seems to list unifying functions of the *renvois*, its last word, *persuasion*, leads us beyond Chambers and beyond unification. In fact, it summons up the role of the *Encyclopédie* as the Enlightenment's great weapon for intellectual subversion. And although some *renvois* contribute to this propagandistic function by linking articles together, others do so by setting them in opposition to one another in such a way as to hold false opinions up to ridicule. These ironic *renvois*, then, opposeront les notions; ils feront contraster les principes; ils attaqueront, ébranleront, renverseront secrètement quelques opinions ridicules qu'on n'oserait insulter ouvertement. (P. 462)

will put ideas in opposition to one another, will contrast principles; they will attack, they will unsettle, they will secretly overturn some ridiculous opinions that one would not dare to insult openly.

The relationship between these two functions of the *renvois de choses* essentially repeats the relationship between the first two *ordres* discussed above. The *ordre général*, it will be recalled, provided the comprehensive, Baconian scheme of knowledge, representing the perspective of mankind, while the *second ordre* consisted of a multitude of conflicting and competing perspectives. By the same token, the *renvois* that unify do so presumably in accordance with the scheme of the *ordre general*, while the *renvois* that bring about ironic clashes of perspectives do so by exploiting the disparate perspectives already embodied in the various articles. These ironic clashes, however, are not merely inherent in the varying perspectives of the articles, but are produced in the service of a further perspective, namely, that of the enlightened and crusading editor Diderot.

The perspective that informs the final sort of significant *renvoi*[22] is again that of the editor, this time, however, not in the role of ironic subverter of superstition, but in the role of scientific and technological genius. These final *renvois* are those

qui, en rapprochant dans les sciences certains rapports, dans les substances naturelles des qualités analogues, dans les arts des manœuvres semblables, conduiraient ou à de nouvelles vérités spéculatives, ou à la perfection des arts connus, ou à l'invention de nouveaux arts, ou à la restitution d'anciens arts perdus. (Pp. 463–64)

which, by bringing out certain connections between the sciences, some analogous qualities between natural substances, some similar techniques in the arts [i.e., all procedures by which humans modify or transform nature], will lead either to new speculative truths, or to the perfection of the arts that we know, or to the invention of new arts, or to the recovery of old arts that had been lost.

Such insights are produced by the sort of man whom we have already encountered in chapter 2, namely, "l'homme de génie" who has "cet esprit de combinaison, cet instinct" (p. 464), which, as Diderot reminds us, he had discussed in *De l'Interprétation de la nature.*

These combinatory *renvois*, then, reflect an intellectual activity distinct both from that which connects articles in accordance with a stipulated scheme of knowledge, and from that which brings about clashes of opposing viewpoints. For these *renvois* cut across conventional patterns of thought in order to provide new connections based on newly discovered similitudes. And although they will not necessarily prove fruitful, "il vaut encore mieux risquer des conjectures chimériques que d'en laisser perdre d'utiles." Thus the inventive activities that in *De l'Interprétation* had been performed by resourceful craftsmen and by scientific geniuses now fall to the man who has studied the procedures of both, namely, the editor.

For Chambers, as we have seen, the disposition of knowledge in the *Cyclopaedia* could not be identical to the microstructure of knowledge as defined by Locke—inasmuch as the articles generally deal with more complex matters than either simple ideas or particulars. However, if a relationship of identity cannot obtain, the overall structure of knowledge as displayed in the *Cyclopaedia* nonetheless bears a *logical* and an *analogical* relationship to the microstructure. If the grouping of particulars is artificial and the work of the imagination, the grouping of phenomena as *belonging* to this or that science or discipline is, by extension, also artificial and arbitrary. And since the features of knowledge in general not only follow logically from the microstructure of knowledge but also resemble the features of that microstructure, the encyclopedic form, with its discontinuous, arbitrary arrangement of discrete articles and its ultimately artificial system or systems of cross-references, is able to represent both at once.

In the case of Diderot's *Encyclopédie*, the particularity of things, the lack of an inherent structure in the universe, gives rise to the multiplicity of perspectives, which, in turn, accounts for the form of the work. Diderot's explanation of the form is thus genetic rather than logical or analogical. But it is not *merely* genetic, and for this reason it is able to establish the representational function of the *Encyclopédie* qua open form. For the various perspectives that produce the form of the work are in fact embodied in it: the human perspective of the general scheme of knowledge, the perspectives of the several authors, of the present state of knowledge in the several branches of learning, the social perspective that determines the amount of scientific and scholarly research that has been devoted to various topics, and finally the diverse perspectives of the editor himself, as imposer of order, as polemical orchestrator of perspectival clashes, as insightful discoverer of unforeseen connections. Thus, although the particularity of things in the universe may be said to generate the diverse perspectives, the perspectives may properly be said to *constitute* the form of the *Encyclopédie.* And this constituting, which at once generates, forms, and informs, yields the ultimate condition of representation, in which re-presentation and presentation are both distinct and identical. The representation that Chambers had stressed, that of a microstructure that resembles the displayed macrostructure, here drops off, and we are left with a form that represents only its own presentation of knowledge. Thus form becomes a representation of itself.

Finally, one cannot recognize the form of the *Encyclopédie* as a structure of perspectives without recalling that Diderot the encyclopedist is also Diderot the dialogist par excellence. In his greatest dialogues, such as *Le Neveu de Rameau* and *Le Rêve de d'Alembert,* one interlocutor does not vanquish another; nor does one, like a Socratic gadfly or midwife, help another to discover truths that he unknowingly had already possessed. Rather, the interlocutors represent opposing intellectual tendencies of the age, irreconcilable tendencies that are embedded in Diderot's own consciousness, and whose conflict can be dramatized but not resolved. The *Encyclopédie,* as Diderot describes it, is just such a dialogue,[23] the most ambitious of all. In it, the greatest minds of the age speak to a public seeking enlightenment as well as to an enlightened posterity; but they also clash with one another and with the benighted voices of the past. Diderot, as editor, mediates between these diverse speakers, through the ordering of articles, through the *renvois,* and through articles of his own composition (including the one whose subject is the encyclopedia itself). He sets interlocutors in conflict with one another, and finds agreements of which they were unaware. He proclaims the unity of the whole and undermines that unity, both in theory and in practice. In so doing the great dialogist manipulates many speakers and speaks with many voices.

Notes

1. *Discours préliminaire,* in *Encyclopédie, ou Dictionnaire raisonné des sciences, des arts et des métiers* (Paris, 1751), 1:36. In these quotations from the *Discours préliminaire* we encounter a problem concerning authorship. The author of the *Discours préliminaire* is, of course, Jean le Rond d'Alembert, who had become Diderot's collaborator in 1749. However, d'Alembert included in his *Discours* a revised version of Diderot's *Prospectus,* which had originally appeared in October 1750. It was in this revised *Prospectus* that the discussion concerning encyclopedic form, from which I quote here, appeared. But not one word of this discussion had appeared in the original version of the *Prospectus.* The changes and additions, d'Alembert announces, "nous ont paru convenables à l'un et à l'autre." This could mean that Diderot wrote the additional material, or that d'Alembert wrote it with Diderot's acquiescence. The radical difference between the tenor of this justification and that of Diderot's article "Encyclopédie," which is examined in this chapter, suggests that the additions were in fact the work of d'Alembert, but I am not prepared to press the point. Instead, I avoid attribution.

2. See chapter 1 above.

3. *Œuvres philosophiques de Buffon,* ed. Jean Piveteau (Paris: P.U.F., 1954), p. 10, col. 2.

4. Ibid., p. 14, cols. 1–2.

5. Ibid., p. 14, col. 1.

6. Ibid., p. 14, cols. 1–2.

7. *Cyclopaedia: Or an Universal Dictionary of Arts and Sciences,* 5th ed. (London, 1741), p. ii.

8. Ibid.

9. Ibid.

10. Ibid.

11. John Locke, *Essay Concerning Human Understanding,* ed. John W. Yolton, rev. ed. (London: Everyman, 1964), bk. 2, chap. 23.

12. Ibid., bk. 3, chap. 3, section 11.

13. In the wake of the medieval realist-nominalist controversy, all anti-realist views, that is, all views that rejected both the Platonic and Aristotelian theories of universals, were called "nominalistic." Technically, however, not all anti-realist views are nominalistic. Locke's view, for example, is generally considered to be conceptualist, which is to say that Locke believed that there are concepts that intervene or mediate between the particulars "out there" and the names by which we group them. (See R. I. Aaron, *The Theory of Universals* [Oxford: Clarendon Press, 1952], chaps. 1 and 2.) Although the distinction between nominalism and conceptualism does not bear upon the present discussion, I shall, in an attempt to be accurate without being pedantic, refer to Locke's position as "anti-essentialist."

14. Aaron, *The Theory of Universals,* p. 37.

15. Locke, *Essay,* bk. 4, chap. 4, section 5.

16. *Cyclopaedia,* p. ix.

17. Denis Diderot, *Œuvres complètes,* ed. Jules Assézat and Maurice Tourneux, 20 vols. (Paris, 1875–77), 14:450–51. Subsequent page references to this article will be given in the text.

18. This passage had its counterpart in the *Prospectus,* from which the two sentences beginning "L'univers ne nous offre que des êtres particuliers . . ." were taken verbatim. Although the language of the passage as a whole, in both versions, clearly betrays the influence of Buffon (and his collaborator, Daubenton), this influence was explicitly ac-

knowledged in the earlier version: "Si l'on ne pouvait se flatter d'assujettir l'histoire seule de la nature à une distribution qui embrassât tout & qui convînt à tout le monde, ce que MM. de Buffon & d'Aubenton n'ont pas avancé sans fondement; combien n'étions nous pas autorisés dans un sujet beaucoup plus étendu, à nous en tenir, comme eux, à quelque méthode satisfaisante pour les bons esprits qui sentent ce que la nature des choses comportent ou ne comportent pas."

19. Chambers, too, had adopted a general scheme of knowledge, the first division of which was between natural knowledge and artificial knowledge. See *Cyclopaedia*, p. iii.

20. The reader will have noticed that I omit Diderot's discussion of the *troisième ordre*, that of "la distribution particulière à chaque partie." "Cet ordre," Diderot tells us, "ne me paraît pas entièrement arbitraire" (p. 457). The individual sciences have their own orderly structures, which Diderot likens to those of trees. (The general principles of a science are its roots, and the subdivisions, its branches.) In addition to having an orderly structure, these particular "trees," rather than conflicting, can be connected to one another in what seems to be a harmonious relationship. But lest it be supposed that Diderot is here departing from the perspectival description to which I have been adverting, it should be noted that this "distribution particulière à chaque partie" is simply a logical function of the *ordre général*, which, as we have seen, represents the perspective of mankind, and which had arbitrarily stipulated an "arbre des connaissances humaines." The reason, then, that the sciences represented have individual integrity and may be connected to one another is that their boundaries and interrelationships have been created at the outset by an arbitrary choice.

21. Diderot is here referring back to his discussion of the nature of language, which had taken place earlier in the article "Encyclopédie." For a discussion that centers, à la Michel Foucault, on this aspect of the article, see Daniel Brewer, "Language and Grammar: Diderot and the Discourse of Encyclopedism," in *Eighteenth-Century Studies* 13 (Fall 1979): 1–19. In characterizing the classical age as the age of classification, Foucault had treated the conflict between Buffon's nominal classifications and Linnaeus's real classifications as a relatively superficial one, both of whose poles are easily contained in the classificatory mode of interpretation (Michel Foucault, *The Order of Things: An Archaeology of the Human Sciences* [New York: Vintage, 1973], chap. 5). Faced with Diderot's perspectivism, and apparently committed to Foucault's scheme, Brewer is forced to see Diderot's position as transitional, as an "intermediary point between on the one hand a static, atemporal and spatial understanding of the world, which characterizes the classical age, and on the other, a dynamic, historical and evolutionary understanding of things," which is characteristic of the succeeding age (p. 12). However, if, as I suspect, the anti-essentialist tendency of the "Classical Age" is in fact more disruptive of classification than Foucault admits, then perhaps Diderot is less transitional than he seems.

22. I omit discussion of Diderot's "renvois de mots," which avoid the repetition of definitions that are germane to more than one article. These efficient renvois do not bear on the subject at hand.

23. For a reading of the article "Encyclopédie" that takes note of the tension between part and whole, and that sees Diderot's conception of the *Encyclopédie* in dialogical terms, but from a point of view rather different from my own, see Christie V. McDonald, "The Utopia of the Text: Diderot's 'Encyclopédie,'" *The Eighteenth Century: Theory and Interpretation* 21 (1980): 128–44.

6

Afterword:
The Historical Question

Sag nicht: "Es *muss* ihnen etwas gemeinsam sein . . ." sondern *schau* ob ihnen allen etwas gemeinsam ist. . . . denk nicht, sondern schau!
— Ludwig Wittgenstein, *Philosophische Untersuchungen*

The open works that have been examined in the preceding pages all date from a period that witnessed the development and consolidation of philosophical schools that stood in opposition to "dogmatism," especially that associated with medieval scholasticism. A major influence in the rejection of dogmatism was the revival of skepticism in the sixteenth century.[1] The skeptics attacked the dogmatists' claims that they could go beyond mere appearances to the essences of things, and those thinkers who sought to develop new philosophies on more solid foundations generally felt compelled to take the skeptical critique of dogmatism into account. The seventeenth-century philosophical outlook that has perhaps had the most profound impact on Western thought is the scientific one, which has been characterized as a "mitigated skepticism," an attempt to find a constructive *via media* between skepticism and dogmatism.[2] And this scientific *via media*—whether it took the form of a hypothetical science of appearances, as in the case of Mersenne and Gassendi,[3] or an experimental method that sought to compensate for the weaknesses of man's senses and reason, as in Bacon[4]—involved a recognition not only of the insufficiency of our present knowledge, but even of the limitations of our potential knowledge.

The British Empiricists of the seventeenth and eighteenth centuries began, as did the skeptics, with appearances, and although they invoked ideal standards of truth and certainty that they may be seen to have shared with the rationalists of the period,[5] such standards were, in effect, derived from the skeptics, whose critiques of dogmatism were aided by rigorous standards of certainty. Thus, although the empiricists sought to account for the appearances, in the process they found themselves impelled to reject various claims to knowledge on the ground that those claims were, in the light of their rigorous criteria, ill-founded. Moreover, according to Locke's influential empiricist psychology, man gathered his sense impressions, upon which all knowledge was based, through a gradual additive process. Some of the major strands of seventeenth- and eighteenth-century thought then were built upon a critical attitude toward claims to knowledge, ranging from the view that man's knowledge was only partial, to the view that knowledge was unattainable.

Now, we have already seen that such views readily lend themselves to representation by discontinuous forms; and the seventeenth and eighteenth centuries in fact witnessed the emergence of numerous discontinuous works. In addition to the texts already discussed in this study, there were poetic and philosophic works that, following the rambling example of Montaigne,[6] were labeled "Essays."[7] There were also such prominent aphoristic works as those of La Rochefoucauld and La Bruyère, and countless narrative works that were, in varying degrees, episodic or digressive. Prose and verse "Anatomies" and various Baroque poems and poems in the Georgic-descriptive tradition exhibit a variety of discontinuous forms.[8] One might also mention such works as Bayle's *Dictionnaire historique et critique* (1697), with its series of notes radiating out from the main text, and similar discontinuous structures of text and notes in such works as Mandeville's *Fable of the Bees* and Pope's *Dunciad*. Even the Augustan heroic couplet may be seen as producing a sort of fragmented poetry consisting of discrete units arranged in inorganic or even arbitrary order.[9] The list of discontinuous literary works in the seventeenth and eighteenth centuries is, in sum, quite substantial.

In view of the resemblances between various new discontinuous literary and philosophical forms and the period's epistemological attitudes, one might be tempted to conclude that the open form as a historical phenomenon emerged concurrently with modern epistemology and, in fact, as a representation of it. But we have already seen (in chapter 1) the dangers of making such claims, for a discontinuous form may resemble any one of a number of things;

and it may resemble several distinct philosophical positions. Moreover, we have already encountered open works whose forms represent philosophical doctrines other than those of early modern epistemology. Thus theory and practice have taught us that, without determining which resemblance, if any, was intended by the author of each individual work, one cannot make claims about what is being represented by a series of works having a similar form.

Now, the sort of procedure whose validity I am attacking is one that is in widespread use, not only among critics concerned with the history of literary forms and genres, but also in the related areas of historical stylistics and the history of style in the fine arts. It is, in fact, so common for critics to assert, merely on the grounds of a general resemblance, that a form or style that was in fashion at a given time reflects a certain contemporary mode of thought, that one might imagine that the procedure has a justification that I have overlooked. For example, it might be objected that just as there are various contexts that can allow us to determine what an individual form represents, there is also a "historical context" that can allow us to interpret entire groups of works.

And indeed, I am not denying the possible usefulness of certain kinds of "historical contexts." For example, if an analysis of numerous discontinuous works from a given time and place revealed that the forms of the works consistently represented a given contemporary viewpoint, then this collection of individual analyses could be seen to constitute a historical context, which could aid in the interpretation of additional works from the same time and place. A work whose individual contexts were in themselves inadequate for a reliable interpretation of its form thus might be tentatively interpreted with the aid of such a historical context.

But in the procedure whose validity I am questioning, it is precisely this historical context that is being posited, not by means of the collection of individual instances, but presumably on the basis of another "historical context." And this other "historical context" is a picture of a contemporary viewpoint that a series of forms are seen to resemble. The trouble with the application of this other historical context to the interpretation of a series of forms is that such a procedure fails to demonstrate that the supposed historical context is relevant, that it is the particular historical context appropriate to the works under consideration. The relationship between a series of forms and a given philosophy or mode of thought is precisely what needs to be established; a mere resemblance does not serve to establish it because the forms may also resemble other possible "historical contexts." Seventeenth- and eighteenth-century discontinuous forms, for example, may be seen to resemble not only contemporary epistemological views, but also such aspects of contemporary thought as the rejection of final causes; the revival of atomism and the accompanying prominence of contingency as a causal principle; the perspectivist metaphysics of Leibniz and its theological counterpart in Lessing;[10] and anti-essentialism, such as we have found in Chambers, Buffon, and Diderot, with its tendency to break down Aristotelian classes into a world of discrete individuals. Each of these trends of thought could constitute an attractive "historical context" on the basis of which one might offer interpretations of discontinuous works. But what guarantees that the historical context that one chooses to invoke is specifically applicable to the works being interpreted? Surely it is not the resemblance, for the resemblance is shared by all the possible historical contexts, and is, in fact, that which gives them their status as possible contexts. The resemblance therefore cannot allow us to choose one possible "historical context" over its rivals.

Nor can we necessarily assume that the problem is simply to determine which one of the immediate historical contexts is uniquely applicable; for a writer may use a literary form to represent older ideas, unfamiliar foreign ideas, ideas that he himself is introducing for the first time, or various combinations of these. We have seen, for example, that the form of Thomson's *Seasons,* although it may be seen to *resemble* contemporary epistemological attitudes, intentionally *represents* the traditional, and perhaps archetypal, cosmological view according to which differentiation constitutes order. And the poem offers as the intellectual counterpart to this cosmological norm, not the additive mode of empiricist psychology, but the analytic mode of thought which, in imitation of the Creation, separates things from one another.

Finally, we must recall that a discontinuous form not only need not represent a single contemporary trend of thought, but that it need not represent anything at all. For as we saw in chapter 1, although the form of a work may resemble many things, it represents only what the author intended. And an author may not have intended his discontinuous form to represent anything at all.

The resemblance, then, between discontinuous works and a possible historical context does not in itself establish the applicability of that context. The task of the critic in this area is precisely to determine whether a historical context that is *possibly* applicable is one that is *probably* applicable. To recognize that a historical context is possibly applicable to a group of discontinuous works is, in effect, to frame a hypothesis about the relationship between the historical context and the literary form, and to determine that this relationship is probable is to confirm the hypothesis. This confirmation can occur only if we go back to the individual works. The procedure that I am advocating is similar to the automatic procedure that we employ in interpreting texts. We move back and forth between the details and our hypothesis as to the overall meaning. Some details may suggest a hypothesis and other details then serve to confirm it. By the same token, our analysis of some individual works from a given period may suggest a historical hypothesis, say a general explanation about the relationship between a given form and a given set of ideas. The notion that the open form arose as a representation of modern epistemological ideas constitutes such a hypothesis. It is suggested by our recognition of certain "details," namely, that the forms of some individual works of the period resemble some ideas that were current at the time. To confirm this hypothesis we need to examine an adequate range of "details," in this case a range of individual works.

But to find that several individual works resemble in their forms the shapes of certain contemporary ideas will not provide adequate confirmation of the *representational* hypothesis because of the gap that we have found between representation and mere resemblance. Thus, to confirm the hypothesis we need to ascertain that the forms of several works not only resemble epistemological ideas, but that these resemblances were intended by the authors. And this requires the accumulation of individual textual analyses carried out in the service of the hypothesis.

What I am suggesting then is not a sort of historical atomism in which we refuse to speculate about the relationship between individual works with similar forms or the relationship between groups of such works and contemporary ideas. I am suggesting merely that we recognize our speculations for what they are— potentially fruitful ideas that may advance our understanding of history but that will effect such an advancement only when they are confirmed or rejected. (For even the disconfirmation of a hypothesis advances our knowledge.) We shall not test our hypotheses, however, if we mistake them for conclusions, if we content ourselves with the attractiveness of our speculations. To alter my epigraph: *Denk, aber schau auch.*

Notes

1. Cf. Richard H. Popkin, *The History of Scepticism from Erasmus to Spinoza* (Berkeley: University of California Press, 1979), chap. 2.

2. Ibid., pp. 103, 132.

3. Ibid., pp. 132–49.

4. Bacon's views on the role of his new organon as a *via media* are described on p. 45 above.

5. Cf. D. W. Hamlyn, *The Theory of Knowledge* (New York: Anchor, 1970), p. 24.

6. A good case for interpreting the form of the *Essais* of Montaigne as an open form representing Montaigne's skepticism has been made by Hugo Friedrich in his *Montaigne* (Bern: A. Francke, 1949), especially p. 430.

7. Locke's *Essay Concerning Human Understanding* and Pope's *Essay on Man* are perhaps the two most prominent examples. For the Augustan distinction between the essay as a "loose and free" form, in contrast to the "Regularity of a Set Discourse," see Addison's *Spectator,* no. 249. This distinction may, I think, be related to Addison's distinction between Nature and Art (see *Spectator,* nos. 414 and 477) and, by extension, to the distinction between the Great (the sublime) and the Beautiful (see *Spectator,* nos. 411–21).

8. For some interesting examples, see Donne's *Anatomie of the World,* Burton's *Anatomy of Melancholy,* Marvell's *Upon Appleton House,* Theophile de Viau's *Ode* "Un corbeau devant moy croasse. . . ," and Góngora's *Soledades.*

9. See Ralph Cohen, "The Augustan Mode in English Poetry," *Eighteenth-Century Studies* 1 (Fall 1967): 3–33. Cf. Donald J. Greene, " 'Logical Structure' in Eighteenth-Century Poetry," *Philological Quarterly* 31 (July 1952): 315–36.

10. See Henry E. Allison, *Lessing and the Enlightenment* (Ann Arbor: University of Michigan Press, 1966), chap. 4.

Works Cited

Aaron, R. I. *The Theory of Universals.* Oxford: Clarendon Press, 1952.

Allison, Henry E. *Lessing and the Enlightenment.* Ann Arbor: University of Michigan Press, 1966.

Arthos, John. *The Language of Natural Description in Eighteenth-Century Poetry.* Ann Arbor: University of Michigan Press, 1949.

Bacon, Francis. *The New Organon and Related Writings.* Edited by Fulton H. Anderson. Indianapolis: Bobbs-Merrill, 1960.

————. *Works.* Edited by James Spedding, Robert Leslie Ellis, and Douglas Denon Heath. 15 vols. Boston, 1861–64.

Bond, Donald F., ed. *The Spectator.* 5 vols. Oxford: Clarendon Press, 1965.

Brewer, Daniel. "Language and Grammar: Diderot and the Discourse of Encyclopedism." *Eighteenth-Century Studies* 13 (Fall 1979): 1–19.

Brochard, V. *Les Sceptiques grecs.* Paris: J. Vrin, 1959.

Buffon, Georges Louis Leclerc, compte de. *Œuvres philosophiques de Buffon.* Edited by Jean Piveteau. Paris: Presses Universitaires de France, 1954.

Burke, Edmund. *A Philosophical Enquiry into the Origin of Our Ideas of the Sublime and Beautiful.* Edited by J. T. Boulton. London: Routledge, 1958.

Cassirer, Ernst. *The Philosophy of the Enlightenment.* Translated by Fritz C. A. Koelln and James P. Pettegrove. Boston: Beacon Press, 1955.

————. *The Philosophy of Symbolic Forms.* Translated by Ralph Mannheim. 3 vols. New Haven: Yale University Press, 1955.

Caws, Peter. "Scientific Method." *Encyclopedia of Philosophy.* 1967.

Cervantes, Miguel de. *Don Quijote de la Mancha.* Edited by Martín de Riquer. Barcelona: Juventud, 1958.

Chambers, Ephraim. *Cyclopaedia: Or an Universal Dictionary of Arts and Sciences.* 5th ed. London, 1741.

Cohen, Ralph. "The Augustan Mode in English Poetry." *Eighteenth-Century Studies* 1 (Fall 1967): 3–33.

————. *The Unfolding of* The Seasons. Baltimore: Johns Hopkins University Press, 1970.

Colie, Rosalie. *Paradoxia Epidemica.* Princeton: Princeton University Press, 1966.

————. *The Resources of Kind: Genre-Theory in the Renaissance.* Edited by Barbara K. Lewalski. Berkeley: University of California Press, 1973.

Diderot, Denis. *Œuvres complètes.* Edited by J. Assézat and M. Tourneux. 20 vols. Paris: Garnier, 1875–77.

————. *Œuvres philosophiques.* Edited by Paul Vernière. Paris: Garnier, n.d.

————, et al. *Encyclopédie, ou Dictionnaire raisonné des sciences, des arts et des métiers.* 28 vols. Paris, 1751–1772.

Dieckmann, Herbert. "The Influence of Francis Bacon on Diderot's *Interprétation de la nature.*" *Romanic Review* 34 (1943): 303–30.

Ducasse, Curt J. "Francis Bacon's Philosophy of Science." In *Theories of Scientific Method: The Renaissance Through the Nineteenth Century.* Edited by Edward H. Madden. Seattle: University of Washington Press, 1960.

Ebner, Dean. *Autobiography in Seventeenth-Century England: Theology and the Self.* The Hague: Mouton, 1971.

Eco, Umberto. *L'Œuvre ouverte.* Translated by Chantel Roux de Bézieux, with André Boucourechliev. Paris: Editions de Seuil, 1965.

————. *Opera aperta: Forma e indeterminazione nella poetiche contemporanea.* Milan: Bompiani, 1962.

————. "The Poetics of the Open Work." Translated by Bruce Merry. *Twentieth-Century Studies,* no. 12 (December 1974), pp. 6–26.

————. *The Role of the Reader: Explorations in the Semiotics of Texts.* Bloomington: Indiana University Press, 1979.

————. *A Theory of Semiotics.* Bloomington: Indiana University Press, 1976.

Eliade, Mircea. *The Myth of the Eternal Return, or Cosmos and History.* Translated by Willard R. Trask. Princeton: Princeton University Press, 1954.

Eliot, T. S. *The Complete Poems and Plays: 1909–1950.* New York: Harcourt, Brace, n.d.

Empson, William. *Seven Types of Ambiguity.* 1930; reprint, New York: New Directions, 1966.

Foucault, Michel. *The Order of Things: An Archaeology of the Human Sciences.* Anonymous translation. New York: Vintage, 1973.

Frank, Joseph. "Spatial Form: An Answer to Critics." *Critical Inquiry* 4 (Winter 1977): 231–52.

―――. "Spatial Form in Modern Literature." In *The Widening Gyre: Crisis and Mastery in Modern Literature*. 1963; reprint, Bloomington: Indiana University Press, 1968.

―――. "Spatial Form: Some Further Reflections." *Critical Inquiry* 5 (Winter 1978): 275–80.

Friedrich, Hugo. *Montaigne*. Bern: A. Francke, 1949.

Gombrich, Ernst. *Art and Illusion: A Study in the Psychology of Pictorial Representation*. 2d ed. New York: Pantheon, 1961.

Goodman, Nelson. "Seven Strictures on Similarity." In *Problems and Projects*. Indianapolis: Bobbs-Merrill, 1972.

Graff, Gerald. *Poetic Statement and Critical Dogma*. Evanston, Ill.: Northwestern University Press, 1970.

Greene, Donald J. *The Age of Exuberance: Backgrounds to Eighteenth-Century English Literature*. New York: Random House, 1970.

―――. " 'Logical Structure' in Eighteenth-Century Poetry." *Philological Quarterly* 31 (July 1952): 315–36.

Guillén, Claudio. *Literature as System: Essays Toward the Theory of Literary History*. Princeton: Princeton University Press, 1971.

Guthrie, W. K. C. *A History of Greek Philosophy*. 2 vols. Cambridge: Cambridge University Press, 1962.

Hamlyn, D. W. *The Theory of Knowledge*. New York: Anchor, 1970.

Hermerén, Göran. *Representation and Meaning in the Visual Arts: A Study of the Methodology of Iconography and Iconology*. Stockholm: Läromedelsförlagen, 1969.

Hirsch, E. D. *Validity in Interpretation*. New Haven: Yale University Press, 1967.

Hobbes, Thomas. *The English Works of Thomas Hobbes of Malmesbury*. Edited by Sir William Moleworth. 16 vols. London: Bohn, 1869.

Hönigswald, Richard. *Vom erkenntnistheoretischen Gehalt alter Schöpfungserzählungen*. Richard Hönigswald: Schriften aus dem Nachlass, no. 1. Stuttgart: Kohlhammer, 1957.

Horton, Mary. "In Defence of Francis Bacon: A Criticism of the Critics of the Inductive Method." *Studies in the History and Philosophy of Science* 4 (1973): 241–78.

James, Henry. *The Art of the Novel*. New York: Scribners, 1934.

Johnson, Samuel, ed. *A Dictionary of the English Language*. 6th ed. London, 1785.

Kahler, Erich. "The Disintegration of Artistic Form." In *Out of the Labyrinth: Essays in Clarification.* New York: Braziller, 1967.

Kropf, C. R. "Unity and the Study of Eighteenth-Century Literature." *The Eighteenth Century: Theory and Interpretation* 21 (Winter 1980): 25–40.

Locke, John. *An Essay Concerning Human Understanding.* Edited by John W. Yolton. rev. ed. 2 vols. New York: Everyman, 1965.

Lovejoy, A. O. *The Great Chain of Being: A Study of the History of an Idea.* Cambridge: Harvard University Press, 1936.

McDonald, Christie V. "The Utopia of the Text: Diderot's *Encyclopédie.*" *The Eighteenth Century: Theory and Interpretation* 21 (Winter 1980): 128–44.

McKillop, Alan Dugald. *The Background of Thomson's* Seasons. 1942; reprint, Hamden, Conn.: Archon, 1961.

McRae, Robert. "The Unity of the Sciences: Bacon, Descartes and Leibniz." *Journal of the History of Ideas* 18 (January 1957): 27–48.

Marshall, Donald G. "Plot as Trap, Plot as Mediation." *Bulletin of the Midwest Modern Language Association* 10 (Spring 1977): 11–29.

Martínez-Bonati, Félix. "Cervantes y las regiones de la imaginación." *Dispositio* 2 (Winter 1977): 28–53.

Milton, John. *The Works of John Milton.* Edited by Frank A. Patterson. 18 vols. New York: Columbia University Press, 1931–38.

Mitchell, W. J. T. "Spatial Form in Literature: Toward a General Theory." *Critical Inquiry* 6 (Spring 1980): 539–67.

Monk, Samuel Holt. *The Sublime: A Study of Critical Theories in XVIII-Century England.* 1935; reprint, Ann Arbor: University of Michigan Press, 1960.

Montaigne, Michel de. *Essais.* Edited by Maurice Rat. 2 vols. Paris: Garnier, 1962.

Nicolson, Marjorie Hope. *Mountain Gloom and Mountain Glory: The Development of the Aesthetics of the Infinite.* Ithaca: Cornell University Press, 1959.

———. *Newton Demands the Muse: Newton's Optics and the Eighteenth-Century Poets.* Princeton: Princeton University Press, 1946.

Ogden, H. V. S. "Variety and Contrast in Seventeenth-Century Aesthetics." *Journal of the History of Ideas* 10 (1949): 159–82.

Orsini, G. N. Giordano. *Organic Unity in Ancient and Later Poetics: The Philosophical Foundations of Literary Criticism.* Carbondale: Southern Illinois University Press, 1975.

Pascal, Blaise. *Œuvres complètes.* Edited by Louis Lafuma. Paris: Editions du Seuil, 1963.

Pepper, Stephen. *World Hypotheses: A Study in Evidence.* Berkeley: University of California Press, 1942.

Pope, Alexander. *An Essay on Man.* Edited by Maynard Mack. The Twickenham Edition of the Poems of Alexander Pope. vol. 3, pt. 1. New Haven: Yale University Press, 1950.

Popkin, Richard H. *The History of Scepticism from Erasmus to Spinoza.* Berkeley: University of California Press, 1979.

Popper, Karl. *The Logic of Scientific Discovery.* New York: Basic Books, 1959.

Russell, Bertrand. *A History of Western Philosophy.* 1948; reprint, New York: Simon and Schuster, 1964.

Sayce, R. A. *The Essays of Montaigne: A Critical Exploration.* London: Weidenfeld and Nicolson, 1972.

Schlegel, Friedrich. *Friedrich Schlegel: Seine prosaischen Jugendschriften.* Edited by J. Minor. Vienna, 1882.

Schwartz, Jerome. *Diderot and Montaigne : The* Essais *and the Shaping of Diderot's Humanism.* Geneva: Droz, 1966.

Thomson, James. *The Seasons.* Edited by James Sambrook. Oxford: Clarendon Press, 1981.

———. *The Seasons and the Castle of Indolence.* Edited by James Sambrook. Oxford: Clarendon Press, 1972.

Tuveson, Ernest Lee. *Millennium and Utopia: A Study in the Background of the Idea of Progress.* 1949; reprint, New York: Harper Torchbooks, 1964.

Weinberg, Bernard. *A History of Literary Criticism in the Italian Renaissance.* 2 vols. Chicago: University of Chicago Press, 1961.

Whitehead, Alfred North. *Science and the Modern World.* 1925; reprint, New York: Mentor, 1948.

Whyte, Lancelot Law, ed. *Aspects of Form: A Symposium on Form in Nature and Art.* London: Lund Humphries, 1951.

Willey, Basil. *The Eighteenth-Century Background: Studies on the Idea of Nature in the Thought of the Period.* 1940; reprint, Boston: Beacon Press, 1961.

Wilson, Arthur M. *Diderot.* New York: Oxford University Press, 1972.

Wölfflin, Heinrich. *Principles of Art History: The Problem of the Development of Style in Later Art.* Translated by M. D. Hottinger. New York: Dover, 1950.

Wollheim, Richard. *Art and Its Objects.* Cambridge: Cambridge University Press, 1980.

Index